How to Manage Money When You're Not Earning Enough

Strategies for Thriving amid financial Difficulties

By

P. A. Simon

First edition: June 2020

ISBN: 9788395683756 (paperback)

ISBN: 9788395683763 (ebook)

Table of Contents

Introduction 9

Chapter I - Understanding your money mindset 13

Why is it crucial to understand your money personality? 16

What is the goal of your money mindset? 21

Changing your money mindset 22

Chapter II - Your spending personality 33

Tips for controlling your spending 38

Chapter III - Automate your financial life 47

Why should you automate your finances? 48

Steps to automate your finances 49

Chapter IV - Paying yourself first 55

Reasons why you should pay yourself first 57

How to cultivate the habit of paying yourself first? 63

For self-employed 64

Chapter V - Cutting down your expenses 67

Keeping track of your spending 68

Learning to spend less than your paycheck 74

Reduce your expenses 76

Chapter VI - Budgeting & financial planning 89

Why do you need to budget your money? 90

Types of family budget 95

Steps to budgeting 98

Managing a budget surplus or deficit 107

Chapter VII - Get out of debt & stay debt-free 111

Understanding the emotional side of saving and spending.... 111

Why you accumulate debt 113

How do you know you have too much debt 115

Get out of debt and gain financial freedom......................116

Develop a plan to settle your debts 121

Chapter VIII - Surviving a recession 127

Chapter IX - Building up your emergency funds................... 139

How much should you have as your emergency fund?..........141

How to use your emergency founds 143

Steps to building emergency funds 145

Chapter X - Building & growing your life savings................151

So, why build life savings.................................... 152

Setting up your savings account........................... 153

Steps to setting up your savings account 155

Maintaining your life saving account 157

Chapter XI - Leveraging technology to manage your finances161

Possible downsides of technology 165

Chapter XII - Investing even when you're not earning enough
.... 171

The best time to invest.................................... 173

Possible ways to invest money 173

How to avoid investment mistakes 176

Final thoughts 181

References 187

About the author 195

"Try to save something while your salary is small;

it's impossible to save after you begin to earn more."

Jack Benny

Introduction

When you search the topic *"financial management"* on Google, you will be amazed at the number of results you get. The topic of money is one that affects every one of us and our ability to manage our funds will determine how comfortable our lives will be. If you must resist the pressures and temptations of living in a society that always demands instant fulfillment, then you need the right information and character. Unfortunately, cultivating the character to resist such temptations is not an easy task because of the human nature that always desires nice things and yearns to live well. For instance, based on available data from Experian's 2019 Consumer Debt Study, the total consumer debt in the United States stood at $14.1 trillion and an average American has an average personal debt of $90,460. This is just the picture of one country and I can assure you that it's no different in other cities around the globe regardless of gender, age or race.

If you must achieve your long-term goal and live a happy and successful life, then you need to learn how to manage your finances effectively. There is no easy and free money anywhere and *"a golden"* advice or ways to get rich quickly doesn't exist. Well, you could be super rich if you win a lottery (which is most unlikely) or inherit the wealth of your rich and lonely aunt that you have forgotten a long time ago. You may also be rich if you were born into a wealthy family where you have all you need in life. But there is really no free money anywhere in the world, you just have to be deliberate about your finances.

I can assure you that this book will not show you tips on how to get rich quickly because they do not exist.

In fact, the quest to get rich quickly has caused many to lose their life savings and plunge into debt while some have even lost their lives due to the pain of losing all that they labored for all their life.

I can assure you that after reading and practicing the strategies I'll be sharing in this book you will get rid of your debts, build a life savings and emergency funds.

You will find tips on how to manage money, create a home budget, manage and plan/track your expenses, automate your finances, thrive amid the global recession and learn various ways to earn, save and invest saved resources. Most of us work hard but only a few earn a lot (Pareto principle?). However, you can organize everything in such a way that you will have enough funds to meet all your needs and even set some money aside for pleasure. Most of the information in this book are not really new, but they are things that most of us have heard before but simply failed to pay attention to them.

There are many books where authorities of the financial market or millionaires present ways to increase their wealth. But the information I'm offering you are the things that have worked for me –

I'm just an average guy like most people out there. I may not have all the money in the world, but I have cultivated simple and common financial strategies that have made me free from debts and with sufficient funds to take care of my family for a long time even without working for months. I'm not afraid of what happens to the global economy because of the sound financial strategies that I have cultivated. I'll be sharing most of the financial strategies that have worked for me over the years and I strongly believe that these strategies for managing money will also work for you.

Ask yourself this question, what is the main difference between the rich and the poor besides assets and account balance?

The rich have a different mindset toward money and they have learned to manage their money well. People who don't have financial problems usually have better money habits. I do not consider myself wealthy, but I am financially free because I can manage my money and this is what I will teach you. If you can't manage your money, no matter how much you earn, you will still end up accumulating debts with lots of bills to pay. One of the most common excuses I hear from people is *"I don't have enough money to manage in the first place."* But this way of thinking is wrong. Did you know that to have more money, you need to first learn to manage the one you already have? No matter how small the amount is, the first step to acquiring assets and obtaining the financial freedom you have always longed for is to manage them. Until you're capable of handling the little you have now, don't expect to get more. Your level of knowledge and money management skills is what makes the difference between financial success and financial failure. Are you eager to acquire money management skills that will help you overcome debt and live a comfortable life? Get ready for an experience of a lifetime!

Chapter I

Understanding your money mindset

My financial situation was in a terrible mess nine years ago and I was practically living paycheck to paycheck. As soon as I earn my monthly pay, all my money would be spent on settling debts and before the next paycheck rolls in, I would have acquired more debts. Sometimes I would wake up in the middle of the night wondering what to do about my money problems. What surprised me the most was that some of my colleagues who earned the same amount of money were living comfortably and even had emergency funds which they rely on when unexpected expenses occur. What were they doing differently? The situation was beginning to affect my health because I was always scared of what would happen if I encounter an emergency.

I didn't like the fact that I was occupied with trying to keep my head above the waters even though I had always desired something bigger in my life – go on vacation, drive exotic cars, and host parties. Well, at that point, I wasn't really interested in buying luxury cars, yacht, or even owning properties in different cities around the globe. My immediate problem was how to offset the debts that had accumulated over the years and stop living paycheck to paycheck. I desperately wanted to live a happy life with the money I was earning but I hadn't a clue on how to go about it. One day, I stumbled upon the quote *"Doing the same thing and expecting a different result is the same as insanity."* I felt so stupid at that point because this was exactly what I was doing – attempting to change my financial status while maintaining my old ways of handling money. Oh, my goodness! If I truly desire to get rid of this debt problem and improve my finances, then I needed to do things differently. So, the question I asked myself was, *"what is that thing I needed to do to gain financial freedom?"* Of course, the answer is to **change the way I handle money – my financial habits and mindset.**

I had earlier tried to increase the amount of money I earn because I reasoned that if I earned more, then I'll have more money to settle my debts, pay my bills and live a comfortable life. Unfortunately, the same habits that caused me to accumulate debt while earning an average salary were still at play in my life. I wasn't making any progress even when I received extra money for a few months. I realized that it was the same factors that were affecting me and not the amount of money I was earning – my poor money management skills. The realization of this problem marked a turning point in my life because I completely overhauled my financial habits after the incident. Although my income didn't increase, I'm now financially free and this was possible because I decided to do things differently. I chose to work on the foundation of financial freedom which is our mind and attitude toward money. The truth is that the achievement of wealth doesn't really depend on the amount of income you have. It comes by deliberately making smart decisions and taking actions toward gaining financial freedom.

We live in a world of duality – hot and cold, fast and slow, up and down, right and left, light and dark, etc. The truth is that for one pole to exist, then the other pole must also exist and there are thousands of opposite poles in every area of our existence. Guess what? It's also impossible for us to have a light side without the dark side! Interestingly, money is not left out in this arrangement – for every *"outer"* law of money, there must also be an *"inner"* law of money. So, I can confidently tell you that the starting point to your financial freedom and ability to manage your money effectively is to understand the laws that govern money. For instance, the outer laws of money include some of the things we will be discussing in this book such as budgeting, building your emergency funds, money management and several others. These things are essential if you desire to gain financial freedom. However, just as these outer laws of money are crucial so are the inner laws. You can have all the right tools required to construct a house, but *"knowing"* the *"right"* tools, resources needed to build the house is also essential.

I have a few questions for you right now;

- Who are you?
- What are your beliefs, habits and traits?
- How do you think?
- What is your money personality?
- How confident are you in yourself and how do you feel deep inside about yourself?
- Do you believe that you deserve wealth?

I can assure you that your level of thinking, your beliefs and character are part of what really determines how successful you are in life and in managing your finances.

Why is it crucial to understand your money personality?

Have you observed that a good number of people who suddenly become rich after winning a lottery or through gambling end up losing all the money? Within a few months or years, they've *"blown up"* financially. Many people who also earned so much money as a result of a sudden boom in their industry or business go ahead to lose it while some that started well failed to end well. What do you think was the cause of their downfall? Let me rephrase this question, what do you think caused me to keep accumulating more debts even when I was earning fairly well? Back to our initial point about two sides to everything. On the outside, it may appear that what caused their loss was a downturn in the economy or bad luck. For me, it could be as a result of a sudden increase in the cost of living and accommodation. Well, there are internal factors also that may be responsible for their loss – their habits and mindsets. This explains why the chances of your wealth may be short-lived and you may lose everything if you suddenly make big money when you're not ready for it.

I also observed that a good number of people don't have the internal capacity to create and retain huge amounts of money as well as the increased number of challenges that come with more success and money. I believe this is the primary reason why such people fail to have much money. This is the primary reason why lottery winners end up going back to their initial financial level – a level they're capable of handling. Research has confirmed repeatedly that regardless of how much an individual may win, lottery winners will most likely return to their original financial state.

Now, let's look at people commonly known as *"self-made"* millionaires. It's interesting to note that most self-made millionaires often regain their financial state even after losing it. A good example is President Donald Trump who was worth billions and at some point, lost everything but regained his money and even made more money several years later. Here is the big question; why does this happen? If you can understand the answer to this question and work toward it, you will certainly be on your way to financial freedom and eventually become an excellent manager of your resources. What differentiates these self-made millionaires who lose everything and later regain them and the majority of lottery winners who eventually lose their fortune and go back to their original state is the *"millionaire mind."* What is the setting of your financial *"thermostat?"* For the likes of Donald Trump, it's set for billions and not millions, but for some people, it's actually set for below zero. Most people are unconscious of their mindset and how they manage their finances.

We all have a kind of blueprint when it comes to money – fixed mindsets that determine what we do with our finances. It's right there in our subconscious mind and it plays a significant role in shaping your financial destiny. What are your thoughts, feelings and actions when it comes to money? That's what your money mindset is all about. For most of us, our money mindset is usually formed from the *"programming"* or information we received in the past while growing up. The main sources of this programming could be our parents, friend, teachers, religious leaders, our culture, authority figures and even our siblings. No child is born with its unique attitude toward money or how to handle money; instead, we're all taught in one way or another. Since we all were taught how to think and act when it comes to money, then it's some kind of conditioning that provides responses that are on autopilot for the rest of our lives. The moment I realized that I had to re-program my money mindset, then I also started making significant changes in the way I handled my finances. I realized that the old programming in me wasn't really serving me properly and I needed a new set of rules. Remember, thoughts will always lead to feelings and feelings will in turn lead to actions that will finally lead to results. So, reprogram your thoughts which is the beginning of your initial programming by adopting new and positive thoughts about money. Most of the things you will be reading in this book will help to change the original programming which may not be serving you well. Once you change the programming, then you also change your thoughts. With the gradual change in your thoughts, you will begin to get a new set of feelings that will lead to different kinds of actions with different and positive results.

When reprogramming your mindset about money, you need to understand how each of us was conditioned. Primarily, we're conditioned verbally through the things we heard while growing up. Also, another way we were conditioned was through modeling and this includes the lessons we learned when we were young. A third and crucial type of conditioning we all had has to do with specific incidents in our lives. What did you experience while growing up that helped shape your attitude toward money?

If you grew up hearing phrases like *"save for the rainy day"* repeatedly, then you may grow up as a *"saver"* instead of a spender. Later we shall look at the different money personalities to help you identify how you spend money. If you grew up always hearing phrases such as *"money talks,"* then you may have the belief that you need to spend money to make a statement. Did you know that most of the statements you heard regarding money while growing up have been stored in your subconscious mind and they end up determining how you behave or handle money? The presence of a negative money mindset often leads to negative emotions like scarcity, overwhelm, despair, and fear. With such emotions, you would rather prefer to ignore your finances because the challenges appear almost impossible to deal with. If you grew up with a mindset that *"money doesn't grow on trees,"* then you end up seeing money as something that's scarce and difficult to get. You will only associate money with evil if you were told while growing up that *"money is the root of all evil."* With such a mindset, you may not be enthusiastic about making money because you believe deep within you that having a lot of money is a bad thing. Another wrong money belief is that *"it takes a lot of money to make money."* Take a look at the life stories of some of the wealthiest people on earth, most of them had humble beginnings and some started small. In fact, in the United States, 88 percent of the millionaires are self-made while 12 percent only inherited their wealth. Wealth creation is similar to building a tower brick by brick, you build it slowly. You don't also need to have a lot of money to make money – a small amount is all you need. You can never successfully manage your finances any if these mindsets exist in your life.

One excellent way to explain the impact of our beliefs (money mindset) on our finances is the relationship between a tree and its fruits. Every tree has fruits and we can also liken our results as our fruits. What helps a tree to produce its fruits is its root – what's under the ground or the things not seen. This also applies to our lives; "*the invisible always creates the visible.*" What creates the fruits on a tree are the seeds as well as the roots of the tree. To change your money mindset, what you need to do is to change the roots – change your beliefs.

I changed my visible (increased life savings, emergency funds, debt-free, etc.) by first changing the invisible (changing the way I see money and believing that I earn enough money to live a good life, developing a budget and changing the way I spend my funds). So, your journey to financial freedom begins from your heart where you transform your money mindsets. You have to start believing that you can live a more fulfilling, wealthy and successful life even when your paycheck is small. Forgive your past financial mistakes and let go of the painful memories and energy field associated with your past. This will prevent you from recreating the same patterns and getting the same results.

Change your story around money and begin to think and say positive things – it's perfectly okay to have abundance, "*I have all I need to live a great life.*" When you have a positive mindset about money, you will gradually begin to believe that it's possible to have abundance. You no longer need to buy things with your money simply to feel better since you're already happy with the little you have. You may feel that what you're earning is so small, just like I once did several years ago, but with the right money mindset, you will discover how blessed you truly are and understand that you can achieve excellent results with what you already have.

Yes, there is sufficient money for everyone who's prepared to get it and you can get it. Get ready to learn more about money so you can manage your finances better. It's not compulsory to start big, just start with what you have – manage the little you're already earning and remember, your financial future is completely up to you. All that's required to create the wealth you've always desired amid the global financial crisis is already inside you. So, get set to learn more as you read further and discover how to do more with the little you have because as you change your money mindset positively and manage the one you have, more money will certainly come your way.

What is the goal of your money mindset?

It's easy to agree that you need to change your money mindset from negative to positive ones. However, what do you hope to achieve by developing a new money mindset? Are you working toward financial success, failure or mediocrity? How are you programmed to behave when it comes to money matters – struggle or ease?

Are you conditioned to live a good life even though you're not earning a fat paycheck or live a good life only when you're having a high income? Are you programmed to have low income, moderate or high income? The best way to discover what your money mindset is set for, is to consider your results. Although I wanted to be wealthy, the money mindset I was having programmed me for mediocrity because my result was neither a success nor failure. So, I was always struggling when it comes to money matters. I believe that as you read further and practice the things you read, you will begin to see results in your finances reflect in your income, bank account, net worth, and the success of your business. You will see results in your money personality or your relationships that involve money and how well you have been able to manage money. The primary reason why I would encourage you to read this book to the end is that your income can only increase to the extent that you grow and improve your money mindset and financial literacy.

Changing your money mindset

Just like every other important thing in life, money management requires a lot of discipline on your part. But the perfect recipe for money misery is the shame and guilt that some people have to deal with in addition to the fact that discipline is not a natural trait in us. Several steps are relatively simple and can help you overcome the negative approach to money as well as lack of financial discipline. These steps will also help you cultivate positive money mindsets and habits. Start by forgiving yourself for all the financial mistakes you have made before. I've made several financial mistakes in the past and it's almost impossible to find someone who hasn't made a mistake before too. Most people have been involved in impulsive buying at some point in their lives while others may have spent their emergency funds on things that weren't so important to them. If you've never made any financial mistake before, then you're definitely going to be the next financial guru. Well, for those of us that have made several mistakes before, this is the time to forgive ourselves. When you forgive yourselves for the mistakes you made in the past, you set yourself free from being a prisoner to your past. This will help to shift your focus away from shame and toward embracing better practices as well as a positive attitude toward money. You just have to acknowledge the errors that you made, apologize to yourself as well as those around you like your partner, then focus on the way forward. According to Brittney Castro, *"Your financial mistakes are not you – your self-worth is independent of your mistakes."*

Clearly define your money mindset

If you must develop a new and positive money mindset, then you have to first evaluate your current thoughts regarding money as earlier mentioned. You need to ask yourself some questions to help you understand how you think and act when it comes to money:

- What are the things you were taught regarding money at home, in school or religious organization?
- How do you value money?
- Do you have future financial goals and if you do, what are the goals?
- What's your spending personality?
- Do you currently have debts and if yes, what are the steps you're taking to pay the debts off?

- If you were to receive 1 million dollars right now, how would you spend it and what are the reasons for your answer?

The truth is that how you value money has a significant impact on how you also generate it in your career or business. Find out the source of each opinion you have about money and what you've learned (including who you learned it from). As soon as you understand the source of your existing money mindset, you also need to examine your spending habit (investor, saver, big spender, or debtor) and I'll be talking about this in the next chapter.

What are your goals for the future? This is another important aspect of your money mindset because you need to set up a clear framework for your financial future which will guide you in your business or career. Please make sure that you answer all these questions as sincerely as possible to help you determine your current money mindset.

Changing your verbal programming

I grew up hearing several phrases that ended up forming my belief about money. I've earlier mentioned some of these phrases and how they influence our lives when it comes to money. After studying this topic for so long, I realized that I needed to change my verbal programming. So, what are some of the things I did to get rid of the old and harmful money phrases in my life? I started by identifying all such statements in my life. Some of these phrases were either restraining me from taking actions toward managing my money effectively or causing me to take the wrong actions. I always believed that the rich will only get richer while the poor keep getting poorer. So, the chances of being wealthy was slim for me, so why try in the first place. I simply lived my life without a definite plan for my finances and ended up in debt. I was also of the view that to make money, I needed to work very hard because money doesn't grow on trees. This also contributed to my decision that there was no point trying to get rich because the rich will continue to get rich while the poor will get poorer. These statements discouraged me from giving my best in some of the things I did after all, *"what's the point trying when things were ordained to go a certain way?"*

If you must get rid of the wrong money phrases that are hindering you, then you need to list all the statements you've heard about wealth and rich people from your parents, siblings, friends, religious figures and others. In your opinion, in what ways have these phrases and statements affected your financial life up to this point in your life?

Once you identify how these statements have influenced your life, go ahead and dissociate yourself from these thoughts. I realized that these thoughts are merely what we learn and completely different from who we are. Every one of us has a choice – we can all choose to do things differently. You don't have to live your life based on the beliefs of others, especially when such beliefs lack value. As soon as you dissociate from these thoughts, then go ahead and embrace new and positive beliefs.

Changing your money mindset through modeling

One of the smartest ways to overcome negative money mindsets is to consider a second way we were modeled while growing up. We were all conditioned via modeling, but have you taken some time to consider your models? The first models we all have are our parents and I learned so much from my dad, but when I engaged in this money mindset exercise, I was amazed to discover that he didn't manage his money well. My father belongs to the category of *"big spenders"* and this influenced my life significantly. One question you need to ask yourself is, how well did my parents manage their money? Were they conservatives or risk-takers? Were they savers, shrewd investors, or non-investors? While growing up, was the flow of money in your home sporadic or consistent? Was money flowing easily in your home or with struggle? Was the topic of finance a source of bitter argument or a source of joy? I realized why it was easy for me to become a big spender because I was doing exactly what I saw my parents do.

Always bear in mind that humans learn almost everything they do via modeling – what we see our parents, guardians, teachers do. Most of us end up being identical to at least one or even a combination of our parents and this is also true in the area of money. My father is of the view that life is meant to be enjoyed, so once he gets his paycheck, our home would be filled with new things ranging from toys, electronics, clothes, especially for my mom, and lots of things to eat. The interesting thing is that toward the end of the month when he had spent most of the money, we would run out of money. Guess what? He would begin to accumulate credit card debts in a bid to provide our basic needs and pay bills. Once his paycheck is ready, he will offset most of the debt and we will be left with some money for our usual spending.

Sometimes, things would be so difficult that my parents would frequently argue over money issues – in fact, the few times they had a heated argument, it was always about our finances. Our debts were piling up; our home was filled with so many gadgets and things we hardly used and if you find yourself in our garage, you may lose your mind. It was filled up with so much stuff and decluttering our home wasn't an option. My parents weren't prepared to let go of all the things they spent a fortune acquiring, but they were occupying so much space in our home. This was my experience while I was growing up and as soon as I was 22, I left home and felt a big relief now that I was going to do things my way. Unfortunately, I was already influenced by my parents and my result wasn't so different from their own. Shortly after I finished school, I picked up several jobs and somehow felt that I needed to furnish my home well. Within three years, I had already purchased so many things that I didn't really need and although I wasn't married; my debts were adding up on a daily basis. But I was fortunate to discover the things I'm sharing with you now on time.

Another thing I'll like to add here is that while some of us are identical to one of our parents or a combination of both in money matters, others also turn out to be the opposite of one or both parents. So, how can you change the wrong modeling from your parents? You need to examine the habits and lifestyle of your parents as well as their money personality. How did your parents behave when it comes to money and wealth? Write down as many as you can remember, then also write down how opposite or identical your attitude toward money is to either of them or both. In what ways did this modeling influence your financial life? Go ahead and write them down. Understand that this approach to money which you learned from your parents isn't you. You actually have a choice to do things differently and manage your finances better than your parents or guardian.

Now commit to doing things not just the way your parents did, but the right way. Commit to practicing the things you've learned and will learn in this book. I can guarantee you that if you can only practice 50 percent of the ideas and information I'm sharing, you will gain financial freedom regardless of how much you earn.

Avoid the comparison trap

I called it a trap because I was once guilty of this mistake. One of the challenges of using social media is the fact that it has given us the chance to project an edited version of ourselves. In the age of celebrity magazines, social media and reality TV, it's not always hard to fall into the trap of comparing ourselves with others. After graduating from school, I got a job I didn't really like for many reasons. But one major reason why I wasn't happy with it was my pay because it could hardly pay my bills. For about a year, things weren't so cool and unfortunately, I was just a fresh graduate with no work experience. One day, I was going through Facebook and the picture of a friend way back in high school popped up. Oh, my goodness, he was sitting on top of a Lamborghini and putting on nice clothes and his skin was spotless. I was carried away by that picture, but things didn't end there as I also saw others who looked so cool. After a few minutes of looking at them, I sighed and dropped my phone; I wondered where I was getting it wrong in my life. How did they manage to achieve all that within a few years? I wasn't really happy with myself and this mood affected my job and personal life for several days. Although I managed to put the thoughts behind me, it would always surface whenever I came across their pictures until I decided to reflect on the whole thing.

I was on my way home when I saw one of the guys I saw on social media, but guess what? He wasn't looking as cool as I had thought when I saw him on social media. I have learned that comparing ourselves to others is one of the worst ways to spend our time. First, when comparing yourself to others, you're simply comparing what you know concerning yourself (everything) to just the little you see about someone else (this is not just the best side of their lives that they choose to showcase, but in most cases, a highly edited version of their best). Do you have an idea about the intimate details of their finances? Have you ever considered the fact that someone can appear to have a wonderful life with luxury vacations, fancy clothes, cars and several others but all that could be courtesy of credit and debit cards or even worse? Always remember that *"all that glitters is not gold."* The first time I saw the picture on social media, it affected my work in the office and even at home for several days. That's one of the challenges of comparing ourselves to others.

Once you begin to compare your life to others and identify the areas you may be lacking, then you're gradually losing focus on your aspirations, plans, and finances. Instead of comparing yourself to others, go ahead and create goals that are attainable for yourself and start comparing yourself to the goals. As you get to certain milestones, make sure that you celebrate your wins and update your goals too.

Embrace positive financial habits

By setting financial goals for your family, you're keeping your eye focused on the prize, but you also need to cultivate the habits to enable you achieve the goals you set. This is where creating a budget that will consider your income and expenses is crucial. A budget will help you to identify areas where you're spending your money and how you can save more which has to be one of your goals. Remember, you need to make the goals achievable (even though they may stretch you a little) so you don't end up getting paralyzed by the size of the goals. Achievable goals will enable you to build on the little achievements as you aim for the bigger goals. The next habit that you need to cultivate is setting aside at least one hour each week for reviewing your finances, how far you've practiced some of the things I'll be sharing in this book and also assessing your progress. Even if you're unable to commit one hour weekly, you can start with 30 minutes and as you get used to it, you may see the need to make it at least one hour as you progress. Just bear in mind that while managing their money, most millionaires spend as much as 8.4 hours monthly. When you calculate the time they spend weekly, that figure translates to about two hours. I always monitor our progress with my partner and I choose weekends to be sure that the two of us are home for the conversation. So, I suggest you involve your partner when managing your finances each week to get the best results. But I must warn you that money discussions often lead to arguments between couples, so you have to also find ways to manage such discussions to get the best results. Another option is to choose one person in your home to be the primary money manager, but it's still crucial for both parties to be on the same page and agree on all goals. It's always easier to delegate money for the different things on the budget when you all have a clear picture of your finances.

Chapter II

Your spending personality

The next line of action that you need to take to help you manage your finances properly even when you don't have enough is to understand your spending style. Your spending style or *"money personality"* just like everything else in life is determined by your personality and modeling. How do you behave when it comes to your finances? The starting point to shaping your approach to spending, saving and investing is to understand your money personality. The focus of this chapter is to help you understand your money personality.

I mentioned earlier that my dad belongs to the *"big spenders"* category and with time, I also learned to spend just like I saw my father do. So, what is your spending personality?

The Big Spenders

Those who belong to this category include the gamblers, adventurers, status seekers, etc. If you love new gadgets, nice cars, and brand-name clothing just like me, then you're likely a big spender.

Spenders are always interested in making a statement and they are fashionable. Here are some characteristics of spenders:

- They hardly have plans for the future and usually live from paycheck to paycheck.
- When going for a shopping spree, you may not have a list or budget. While individuals who belong to other categories such as the savers are searching for the best deals, spenders are mainly interested in the latest and trendy products.
- If you find yourself in debt mainly because you spend impulsively in a bid to be seen as trendy, then you're a spender.
- Do you enjoy purchasing gifts for others or are you fond of buying several rounds at happy hour? Well, if the answer is yes, then you're definitely a spender.

So as a spender, you always love the excitement of purchasing anything you want when you want it. Unfortunately, impulsive spending often leaves you with so many regrets as well as the clutter that's associated with buying the things you don't really need. I was always scared of going to our garage while living with my parents because it was cluttered with stuff that we didn't really need. The truth is that as a spender, you may likely be in debt due to too much spending. Apart from impulsive spenders, there is also another group of spenders known as *"experience spenders."* Those who are regarded as experience spenders love spending their money on exciting trips and events than on items they can retain after using.

Savers

I guess you already understand what it means to be a saver. This is the opposite of the first group of money personalities. Do you always close the refrigerator door immediately just to keep in the cold? Are you always fond of turning off the lights the moment you exit your room? Do you rarely buy things with credit cards or only shop when necessary? Well, if you answered yes to any of these questions, then you're definitely a saver. Savers don't always have debts and are sometimes seen as cheapskates. You're not concerned about going with the latest trends and you're more satisfied when you see the interest in your bank statement than purchasing a new car or gadget. Here are other characteristics of savers:

- Savers would do anything within their power to pay off all bills on time and would avoid being in debt at all costs.
- Savers often have a plan for their future and allocate their funds to handle future expenses
- If you're organized with a good budget and you adhere to your budget without tampering your savings to buy something you don't really need, then you're a saver.
- Savers are always careful with the way they make use of their resources. If you prefer to spend time searching for the best deals before you buy something, then you're a saver.

Savers love socking away sufficient nuts that can last them through winter. This often provides lots of comfort to savers mainly because they are concerned about the future. They always make plans for unexpected costs and most times; their financial decisions often align with their future goals. Watching the steady increase of their funds in a savings account, retirement funds or bank statement is sexy and they love automating their finances.

Debtors

Those who have this kind of money personality are not trying to make a statement when spending money just like spenders or shoppers. They are not often interested in entertaining or cheering themselves up. People who have this kind of personality have simply failed to spend some time thinking about money. So, they fail to monitor what they spend or where they spend their money.

If you're a debtor, then it's most likely that you spend more money than you earn and you end up deeply in debt. Also, you might not be investing your money in any meaningful project and you may even miss taking advantage of great investment opportunities that come your way. Those who have the debtor personality can also be called *"avoiders"* since they don't see the need to learn about their finance. If you are more interested in immediate gratification than the long-term payoff, then you're certainly a debtor or avoider. You may feel overwhelmed by the financial information and end up experiencing what's known as *"analysis paralysis."* which further prevents you from learning about personal finance. Well, at least you're reading this book, and this is the right step in the right direction.

Another common trait among debtors or avoiders is that they hate dealing with bills and setting up an autopay is usually challenging.

You may see money education as something for the bankers, celebrities, famous athletes or wealthy CEOs. So, are you an avoider? Does any of these things happen to you? If yes, then you need to take some steps to address it. We shall look at simple steps you can take to manage your finances better.

Investors

The name already points you to its meaning – individuals who are conscious of their money and fully understand their financial situation. Investors understand the importance of putting their money to work for them. The ultimate goal of investors (regardless of their present financial situation) is to get to the point where they can settle all their bills with the money they get from their passive investments. The actions of individuals who have this kind of money personality are primarily driven by careful decision-making. Also, their investments reveal their desire to take a certain level of risk in their quest to meet their goals.

One of the things you need to do to change the way you handle money is to understand your money personality. Once you know how you handle money, then you know the necessary changes to make to improve your finances. So, which of these personality types best describes? Are you a spender, saver, avoider or investor? How do you approach money and what are the changes you need to make to enable you make the best use of the limited funds you get? As a spender, consider seeking long-term value instead of short-term satisfaction. Just before you begin to spend your money on trendy things, you should pause for a moment and ask yourself how much is this purchase really going to mean to me this year? If it's not much, then you just have to skip it.

You can begin to think long term by channeling your energy into savings. Focus more on slow and steady gains instead of high-risk and instant gratification scenarios. We shall be discussing more on how to increase your savings in chapter ten. As an avoider, you need to expose yourself to financial information, especially if you're often intimidated by certain financial terms. You will become more financially enlightened by the time you're through with this book.

Tips for controlling your spending

Understanding your spending personality is great, but you need to identify simple ways to overcome the challenges associated with your spending personality. Once you have a clear picture of your daily, weekly and monthly spending, then you can make informed decisions on areas you need to make adjustments. So, here are some tips to help big spenders and debtors have better control of their income.

1. Spending only cash

Studies have revealed that people seem to spend less when making use of cash. You may create a perfect budget, but if you fail to stick to it, then it's merely a Wishlist. Spending only cash is an excellent way to compel yourself to live within your means – at least for some time.

One of the benefits of using cash only is that it enables you to get a visceral experience of seeing and feeling the money you're spending. Another benefit of spending cash only is that you will be compelled not to spend above your means if you don't use debt. You can automate payments into your savings account as well as a separate checking account where you also automate the payment of your bills. Now, you can simply restrict yourself to spending the remaining cash in your account. I'll be sharing more about how you can automate your finances later.

2. Consider leveraging the envelope system

Some people make use of the envelope system to help them stick to their budget and avoid exceeding their monthly spending limit. So how does the envelope system work? It requires you to put the different categories of cash you want to spend for the month in different envelopes. Have an envelope for kids' activities, clothes, groceries, etc. As soon as the cash in an envelope is finished, then you won't spend again for the specific category until the next month. You can even take advantage of some apps that enable you to utilize a virtual envelope system such as **Mvelopes**. Try the Virtual envelopes to see if they are effective in restricting your spending just like physical envelopes.

3. Practice the 24-hour rule when making a purchase

Online shopping has made it easy for us to buy almost anything with our smartphones or computers. It was one of the reasons why I bought so much stuff that I didn't need and as soon as I finished paying for an item online, I would be full of regrets and realize that I had almost exhausted my money for the month. Although I didn't use all the tips I'm sharing, some of them were extremely helpful and one of them is observing the 24-hour rule. Before buying anything online, the rule for me is to add the item to my cart and leave it for at least 24 hours. Well, I often cancel the request the next day because 24 hours is enough for me to consider how useful the item was to me. With time, I began to make better decisions even without waiting for 24 hours. If your money personality is *"Big spender,"* then instituting a 24-hour rule when making any purchase will help prevent you from impulsive buying. This strategy will force you to delay for 24 hours before buying anything. With this rule, you increase the chances of buying only the things you genuinely want. When it comes to the 24-hour rule, there are different approaches. For instance, you can establish a basic threshold and agree that once a purchase exceeds $60, then the rule will apply. You can also agree that for every $100 cost of an item, you will require a full 24-hour period before making the purchase. This implies that if you're buying an item worth $400, then you will need at least four days before finally deciding whether to proceed or not. Embracing this rule will not only help you buy the items you truly want, but it will also give you time to search for the best price and quality of the product or service.

4. Don't shop when you're hungry

Most times when we visit the grocery store hungry, we always purchase many things impulsively. In addition, when you shop while being hungry, you are also very vulnerable to overconsumption.

According to researchers, it was observed that a hungry department store shopper spent as much as 60 percent more buying "food products" than other shoppers who were not hungry. Make sure your belly is full before heading to the grocery store.

5. Establish no-spend days

Perhaps one of the benefits of the COVID-19 lockdown season is that most people had to stay home to avoid getting the virus. But it also helped people cut down on their expenses. If you're searching for an excellent way to reduce how much you spend, then simply choose not to buy anything at all. Well, it's also impossible to do this forever; however, it's possible to create no-spend days every month or set aside one full month as your no-spend month.

Once you've agreed on a specific day, then commit to buying nothing on those days. But if you choose a no-spend month, then you can only purchase nothing else but absolute necessities like food which you can make at home. You can even take it a step further by making it fun. See how many no-spend days you're able to observe in a month and get your partner involved. Have a prize for the person who had the highest number of no-spend days.

Obviously, observing no-spend days helps you to save money since you're simply keeping your wallet and credit cards away, but there are other benefits as well. Perhaps the most significant benefit of the strategy is that it helps you to change your mindset about spending over the long term. This is one of the best tools for "spenders" to break free from the habit of spending more than they earn because observing no-spend days will change your spending habits and help you learn new and creative ways to meet your needs instead of just purchasing new things every time.

6. Endeavor to shop with a list

If you belong to the group for "big spenders," then shopping with a list of the items you want to buy is another excellent way to stop impulse buying. Well, having a list is one thing but you also need to stick to your list. This strategy is not only limited to grocery shopping; you can also use it when buying other things. So, if you desire to buy some clothes and a nice shoe, then consider writing them down on a piece of paper and never allow other things to distract you when buying what you've written down.

7. Delete your credit card details from online accounts

Most online accounts can store credit card details to make checking out easier for customers. I needed the services of a plagiarism checker several years ago, so I paid for a month subscription. Well, after making use of the service, I forgot to delete my credit card details or even stop recurrent billing. I woke up one sunny morning and got an alert on my phone. I was so annoyed to discover that they had already billed me and I wasn't going to use their service for some time. Most of us have experienced something like this with recurring subscriptions. I know it's not always convenient to re-enter your details whenever you're buying something online. But guess what? That inconvenience you're experiencing is the whole point here. When re-entering your information is stressful, then it also reduces the chances of making a purchase. This is because you'll need to grab your wallet, fish out your card and enter all the details. Sometimes, you may omit a number and will have to repeat the process again before hitting the "buy now" button. Repeating the whole process every time you want to buy something will help reduce the possibility of making a purchase.

8. Use the one-in/one-out rule

Chances are than our home is gradually being cluttered with things we don't really need. Most times, we don't need all the gadgets, tools and items in the world to live a comfortable and happy life. This is one of the reasons why I love the minimalist lifestyle – living with less clutter at home and in our lives. But how do you ensure that you're not buying the things that you don't genuinely need?
Establishing the one-in/one-out rule in your home can help you halt the purchase of unnecessary items. Once you embrace this rule, then you will immediately get rid of an old item whenever you buy a new one. So, if you want a new pair of shoes for instance, then an old pair will have to go. If your shoes aren't worn out or bad, why do you want to buy new ones?

I'm certain this rule won't work for all the purchases you make daily, but it's effective because it helps you to make better buying decisions. What do you do with some of the items you're taking out? You can donate them or even organize garage sales to help cover the cost of the new items you want to buy. This strategy will not only help to limit the things you buy but will also help to prevent clutter in your home.

9. Examine your total cost of purchase

Some of the items we buy also have ongoing costs of maintaining and using them. For instance, when we purchased our second car (which was an expensive car), the cost of maintenance of the second car was higher than the first one. We had to pay more on insurance and the car parts were more expensive. This applies to some of the things we buy like a single-cup coffee maker which also requires little cups that can fit in them. When making a decision to buy any item, you need to consider what it will cost to maintain and operate it before you commit to a lifetime of big spending. Are there versions of the item that are cheaper to maintain? If yes, then go for alternative products.

Finally, you may need an accountability buddy to help you stick to your budget as well as lifestyle changes that will help you cut down on your expenses. Shortly after having the discussion with my partner, she agreed to cut down on the number of new clothes she was buying every month. But my wife loves shopping and every time we're in the mall, she's always excited. I knew I had to help her stick to her decision, so we made a deal to always support each other in our efforts to trim our expenses and it was an outstanding idea because it really worked. Your partner can be your accountability partner; it could be your friend, fiancé, a parent, brother or sister. Having an accountability partner doesn't imply that the person will chastise you anytime you slip up. But the purpose of getting someone else involved is to have someone you can report to on how well you're doing with your new decisions. The chances of breaking your spending limits will significantly reduce when you know you have someone who's rooting for you.

I'm sure you may not embrace all the techniques I've just shared, but applying the ones that you feel comfortable with will help you cut down on how much you spend. It will be easier to achieve your financial goals by reducing your outflow and properly directing more of your funds to achieve your financial goals. Based on my experience, the biggest hurdle is not in the number of things you may get rid of in your life but our mindset. We often feel that we deserve nice things since we worked for the money. Well, we only end up making our life uncomfortable with our money and get into debt in a bid to satisfy our ego and the cycle continues to grow strong. Once you're able to understand your *"big goal,"* then cutting your monthly expenses wouldn't be difficult.

Chapter III

Automate your financial life

Have you noticed that the government is smart enough by figuring out how to make you automatically pay them first? Just before you get paid by your employer, your tax needs to be deducted and remitted to the government of your country. So, if the government is smart enough to make you pay them automatically first, why don't you embrace the same strategy? In fact, it's possible to use the exact technology they are using to pay yourself first before you pay the government. It's not rocket science; it's not in any way complicated. All it takes is for you to make use of your smartphone and pen. Technology has indeed made it easy to monitor your finances since you can carry out financial transactions with mobile bank apps on your smartphone. So, it's easy to check your balance and go through all the transactions that took place at home. You don't really need to see paper money or check to carry out a transaction.

Why should you automate your finances?

One of the things you enjoy when you automate your finances is that it helps to make things go smoothly with your funds. You don't have to bother about sending a check when you automate the payment of your bills. In fact, you don't need to worry about your check getting lost in the mail since everything is done online. If you're a spender, then one of the most effective strategies for saving money is to automate your finances. You don't need to remember to move your funds to a savings account when it's automatically put into your savings which could be via automatic transfer or paycheck. Everything takes place on schedule to help you build up your savings regularly. The truth is that when you have cash in hand, it's often challenging to refrain from spending your savings on things you didn't add to your budget. It's usually easy for you to adjust your deposit to suit your spending on things you don't really need. But when you set up regular and automatic deposits into your savings, you can conveniently overcome such temptations. Scheduling automatic payments for recurring payments helps to save you from the negative consequences of failing to make payments on time. Such consequences could be late fees as well as other penalties that may apply to a particular account. Automating the payment of your bills helps to prevent possible errors. Since you can also automate the settlement of your bills, there wouldn't be a need to bother about the payment of your bills even when you're away on vacation. This also takes away a lot of stress out of your life and finances.

Although automating your finances is crucial, you also need to be careful when doing it. It's crucial to have sufficient amount of money in your account when it's time to pay your bills. Sometimes, your payment may eventually go through (with or without sufficient funds in your account) however, you will only end up with overdraft charges. You may end up with accumulated fees when your payment fails to go through. So, how do you effectively automate your finances?

Steps to automate your finances

Start by writing down your pay and how often you receive your pay which could be weekly or monthly.

Simplify your bills

Next, add all your recurring monthly bills. This includes things like memberships, credit cards, tuition costs, subscription, utilities, mortgage, etc. To help you save yourself of the stress of worrying whether you've paid your bills or not. You can even automate your rent by asking your landlord or building manager if it's okay to set up an automatic electronic payment of your rent. The bills you're adding here should be the monthly bills, so don't add variable expenses such as gas and groceries.

It's possible to simplify your bills and ensure that you receive all your bills around the same time each month. If this isn't the case, then you can call each company and request for your bills to be sent at a particular date you feel comfortable with. This is an excellent way to receive all your bills around payday. So, if you receive your paycheck on the first of each month, then you can request to have your monthly recurring bills sent close to the beginning of each month. On the other hand, you can request for your bills to be sent close to the middle of the month if you're expecting your paycheck on the 15th of the month. What if you're always paid twice each month? There are two options available. First, you can decide to receive your bills on the first of every month. You're already aware of your monthly cash flow, so you can avoid overspending between paychecks. Another option is to split up your bills between paychecks so you can receive half of your bills on the 1st of the month while the second one arrives on the 15th.

- Write down all your annual expenses like car registrations, taxes, etc.

- Decide on how much you would spend on unexpected expenses that occur frequently. Examples of such expenses are purchasing a new smartphone, making repairs, etc. Then choose when you want the money to be deducted – a specific amount every paycheck or a monthly deduction.

- Choose one crucial goal you need to handle. Depending on your financial status: if you're indebted, then your essential goal should be to settle your debt. Your goal should be to set aside at least a minimum of three months emergency fund if you're currently debt-free. Your goal should be to invest wisely if you're debt-free and already have a minimum of three months emergency funds set aside.

- What's the amount you desire to devote to the particular goal you have? Choose the right amount based on how much you earn and the amount of debt. For instance, the amount I save toward my goal (which is investment) is $300 per paycheck.

- You may need to open a second checking account if you have just one account with direct deposit. The reason why you need to open a second checking account is to enable you move your bills money away from your hands. So, the second account will be a *"bill payment"* account.

- Once you've listed all your recurring expenses and bills, then go ahead and automate the entire process. First, set up automatic transfer of the amount required to pay all the monthly bills per paycheck to the new checking account every payday. Then all the recurring bills will be paid from the new account. This process might be challenging at first, but over time, it will make your life less stressful for you.

- Does your bank support multiple savings account or *"sub-savings accounts?"* Choose a bank that has such a feature if your bank doesn't support multiple savings account. Go ahead and create separate savings account for annual expenses, then automate recurring payday transfers. So, you can transfer each bill to its separate account like tax money into a tax savings account and the same for others.

- Earlier, I mentioned three different goals you can choose – paying off debt, saving or investing – so set up your final payday recurring transfer based on the goal that applies to you. Transfer money to a separate account if it's an emergency fund or life savings. Other possible savings goals you may need to set aside some money for include: wedding expenses, down payment on a future home, money for a new car, college tuition, and a big project or purchase. If your goal is to offset your debts, then your money should be transferred to wherever you need to send it like your credit card. If your goal is to invest, then the next steps will apply to you.

- Start by choosing the best investment vehicle in your country. For instance, in the United States, you can choose to increase how much you contribute to your 401(K) to the percentage offered by your company. Don't forget that it's free money, so take advantage of this opportunity. What if you're unable to meet up with the percentage? Start with what you can afford right now and increase it once you get a raise. The idea here is to invest in a credible investment vehicle and please avoid schemes that promise you outrageous returns on investments because most of them are scam and you'll only lose your money. Now, you also have to automate the process of transferring your contributions to investment accounts.

- Finally, remember I mentioned that you can increase the amount you invest, well, you can also automate the process of increasing your investment transfers over time. However, this process requires some kind of work but this depends on where the savings are going. some investment platforms and online banks can allow you to increase your recurring contributions each year. This option is helpful when you get a raise because your investment contributions will increase just as your paycheck also increases. The reason why you need to also automate the increase in your contribution is to avoid the influence of lifestyle changes that may suddenly spring up when your salary increases.

What next?

Here is where you begin to experience the benefits of automating your finances. As soon as you've set up this whole process, all the amounts you specified for different purposes – annual expenses, bills, savings, etc., will be deducted and transferred to the separate checking account. Now, the amount that's left in your primary checking account after all the deductions is known as your *"Guilt-free spending money."* This is money you're free to spend and at this point, you just have to figure out the right amount that's safe to spend. You can spend the money left in your checking account on variable expenses as well as things you desire to have. With this strategy, you will gradually offset your debts if you have debts to pay and you can easily pay your bills whenever they are due.

Before I finally decided to automate my finances, I was always struggling to pay my bills, settle my debts and I wasn't making any tremendous progress in my savings. I already knew that it was possible to automate my money, but I never gave it a thought. Well, when I noticed that my paycheck (though not much) is sufficient to cover my bills and make a decent saving, I decided to embrace the process. This is a perfect system for me because it was easy for me to justify purchasing anything that I like. Once I automated my money, all funds were deposited automatically to different accounts so I stopped worrying about having sufficient funds to settle my bills. I was just concerned with how I spent my free money and once it's exhausted, I simply manage what I have until the next payday.

Chapter IV

Paying yourself first

While growing up, I often handled money the way most people would do – purchase the things I wanted, made the trips I loved and made a little effort to save while believing that everything would end up working out for the best for me. Unfortunately, things failed to work out well as the debts were fast accumulating and when I look back at my experience, I wasn't surprised at the result I got back then. The truth is that I wasn't really poor and I was raised in a family that was doing quite well financially, though with a *"big spender"* father.

After obtaining my degree, I got a good job and earned more than enough money to meet my needs. But my lack of planning caused me to get poor results in my finances because I was spending haphazardly and believing that I would still have some money left to settle a debt or save. But when I realized that what I was doing wasn't working (with my debt not reducing and no meaningful savings) I knew I needed to do things differently. I have always been passionate about financial management, so I decided to research and come up with how best to resolve my financial challenges. One of the lessons I learned was cultivating the habit of paying myself first. It's actually one of the pillars of personal finance; in fact, most financial planners are of the view that it's the golden rule to managing your finances effectively. Did you know that in the United States, 60 percent of people don't have sufficient money (savings) to pay for a $1,000 expense if it were an emergency? This was revealed by Bankrate. This golden rule of personal finance is what will set you apart from individuals who just manage to survive every month even when they are earning enough to live a meaningful and comfortable life. It's a rule that requires a little bit of dedication and a great deal of discipline on your part to accomplish.

So, what does it mean to pay yourself first? In simple terms, it means that before you decide to upgrade your phone, go for happy hour drinks with friends, pay your utilities, or purchase a new shirt, set aside part of your income in a savings account or even an investment account. If you choose to pay for most of the things you need such as utilities, groceries and rent, then you may not have enough left to set aside for savings until you get your next paycheck. Unfortunately, if you don't cultivate the habit of paying yourself first, then this cycle will continue. This is one good way to see your savings plan as part of the bills you need to settle regularly. If you automate the process of paying yourself first, then you will certainly build significant wealth. Setting up automatic deductions for this purpose will over time become normal and you wouldn't even notice that a specific amount is being withdrawn from your paycheck. Once you start with an amount you're comfortable with, you can take it a step forward and increase the amount.

Reasons why you should pay yourself first

One of the mistakes that most people make is to save what's leftover after discretionary spending. But there are many benefits you stand to enjoy when you embrace the habit of paying yourself first.

It helps you to set proper priorities

Your future as well as that of your family is perhaps one of the most important things you need to consider. So, what are the priorities that dominate your family's long-term financial security? When you pay yourself first, you also establish a mindset that's an essential aspect of successful saving – my family and I matter and I'm going to act accordingly. Undoubtedly, living a comfortable life and even building wealth with little resources doesn't just happen by chance; instead, it's a result of consistency, intention, big-picture thinking and discipline. This is what paying yourself first helps you to achieve.

It's not difficult to pay yourself first

Once you automate your finances as discussed in the previous chapter, then the money you pay yourself will be deducted automatically. It's simply a *"set it and forget it"* approach to savings and investment since you can direct your funds to a 401K, IRA savings account or any meaningful and credible investment vehicle in your country. Automating the process prevents you from engaging in that *"naggings"* sense of deprivation which has significantly affected the best financial intentions of many people negatively.

Superior strategy for "Spenders"

Remember we earlier talked about our money personality and one of them is "big spenders." This is the name for individuals who only save what's leftover after spending on other things and paying bills. The truth is that new wants and needs will certainly find a way to creep in and they will always consume any surplus available. So, if you're a spender, one of the best strategies you can embrace is to learn to pay yourself first and also automate the process. When you do this, then you have also succeeded in placing savings and investment on top of your financial plan and you will gradually begin to learn to manage the remaining funds you have. This is indeed a superior strategy that will ensure you do more rewarding things with the money you earn (whether big or small).

Have you ever wondered why most experts suggest that we exercise first thing in the morning every day? The reason is not for physiological reasons because our body doesn't really function at its peak early in the morning. But the main reason why they recommend exercising first thing every morning is for psychological reasons. Think of it; we live a busy and engaging life with so much stress during the day. This implies that we may not really have the time to exercise as much as we should. Consider a scenario where you wake up in the morning, prepare as usual and go to work then face the stress and demands of work for the day. After work, you may face serious traffic as you drive back home and finally need to visit the gym. In fact, sometimes, you may have reasons to stay in the office much longer than you should just to complete your job for the day and end up going home late. You may have kids to pick up from school or soccer practice; you may even need to run errands and handle other tasks. How would you go home late and still exercise after all these activities? Well, the answer is obvious – you'll simply continue to procrastinate until you fail to do it all together. This is why most experts recommend that people focus on exercise first thing each day. Guess what? The principle of *"paying yourself first"* also runs on this concept. Attempting to pay for all the other things you need before saving leads to poor savings because you are likely going to end up with nothing. When you save first before paying your bills, then you will compel yourself to make ends meet.

Discipline

When you cultivate the habit of paying yourself first by contributing a specific amount of money to your retirement and savings account, you're also building real *"financial discipline."* Interestingly, you can also apply this kind of discipline to many financial and nonfinancial matters. Just like every other habit that we learn, this habit will ensure that savings will be easier over time. In fact, you may begin to search for ways to cut back on your expenses as you watch your wealth grow gradually and this will in turn further increase your income and investment.

Ensures a healthy work-reward cycle

Have you observed that modern life is actually an endless cycle where we all have to work, spend what we've earned and repeat the entire process? Well, that's what really happens but I also discovered that paying myself first has helped me to balance this cycle. It's an effective way to overcome this work-spend-repeat cycle and even grow your wealth. By paying yourself first, you're creating a new cycle – a cycle where all your hard work results in an increase in your net worth, increase in opportunities and provides you with a freedom that more work can't really provide.

Best way to model smart financial strategy

Most people feel that it's not always the best to burden kids with adult worries like financial matters. Well, I've always strongly believed that it's a smart thing to discuss money with kids. Explaining effective money-saving strategies such as paying yourself first, living within your means and staying away from credit card debt is immensely valuable. When you encourage a certain level of financial transparency, you demystify the world of personal finance and in turn, help your children to cultivate practical money management skills. Well, this is one skill that will serve them well even as adults.

Example

I remember how the strategy of paying self first helped one of my friends several years ago. James is my childhood friend and we actually attended the same school but shortly after graduating, we moved to different cities and over time, things became a bit difficult for him. So, he decided to share his challenges with me. At this point, I had already learned several financial principles and one of them was paying myself first. I had also managed to clear my debts and create an emergency fund for myself. So, this encouraged him to seek my advice. I didn't waste time explaining it to him and even though he didn't initially believe what I was suggesting was going to help him out, he agreed to try it. So, we agreed to meet and look at his finances. James earns about $6,000 each month and has a wife and two children. Well, after the tax deductions as well as the deductions for retirement and insurance, he ends up with just $4500. *"So, what do you do when you're paid every month?"* I asked as we started brainstorming on how best to help him do more with his earning. Once my insurance, retirement and tax deductions have been made, I have house payment of about $1100 as well as $750 car payments to make each month. *"Well, that's not bad at all,"* I replied.

"Okay, so what do you do with the rest of your money," I queried further. I spend about $1,200 on food and we actually dine out a lot leaving us with $700 to spend on different things – entertainment, a new smartphone, remodeling projects, etc. So, at the end of the month, all my earnings are gone and sometimes, I even add to my credit card balances. I examined what James said and based on what he told me; this was how the spend his monthly income:

- Mortgage - $1100
- Credit cards - $470
- Cable and internet - $130
- Car repayments - $750
- Gas, entertainment and miscellaneous - $650
- Food and dining - $1200

Total $4300

Obviously, he didn't make any provisions for his savings but according to him, there were months he spent even more money than he earned which increased his debts. Now I understand why he was finding it hard to offset his debts and live comfortably with the money he was earning. James belongs to the *"Spenders"* category, so he often spends on all other things before considering any kind of savings.

Just like I mentioned earlier, the best way to manage your finances effectively as a spender is to pay yourself first. A look at his expenses revealed that he needs to first cut his food spending since it was obviously outrageous and they were dining out a lot. James never had a budget for his home, so he was just caught up in a cycle of spending more than he earns without even having a life savings. So, he needed to come up with a budget and cut all the extra spending in his family. In fact, he needed to cut down on the number of times they went out to eat instead of eating at home. It was also crucial that they prioritize debt repayment and savings instead of just treating them as an option. These are painful truths that he needed to learn, and it was obvious that he needed to be more financially disciplined. The first thing I asked him to do was to have an open mind and see things differently. It's important to create a new list and a budget to help control how they spend money in his home. I suggested some of the changes he needed to make with the way they spend money. So, here is what we came up with after looking at various ways they spend:

- Savings - $280
- Mortgage - $1100
- Credit card - $900

- Food and dining - $480
- Car repayment - $750
- Gas, entertainment and miscellaneous $250
- Cable and internet $50

Total $4300

Now, more money was channeled toward credit card payment to help him settle his debts and we cut down on what they were spending on food and dining without affecting the quality of food they were eating. Now, if you look at the list of expenses, the first on the list was money set aside to pay himself. The goal of making the adjustments was to help him pay his debts and have some emergency funds which is essential for every family. Interestingly, he managed to implement the new plan and was able to pay off the remaining balances on his cars. Apart from being completely debt-free within a few months of implementing this new strategy, James also started saving a lot more and this boosted his retirement savings. But what excited him the most was the fact that it enabled him to live a stress-free lifestyle without debts or the fear of not being able to handle possible emergencies. Paying yourself first helps to build your financial discipline and this will end up influencing other aspects of your life positively.

How to cultivate the habit of paying yourself first?

It's usually difficult to embrace the "pay-yourself-first" mentality. We all experience that unwillingness to do things differently, especially when we're used to doing it in a particular way since we were born. It's similar to challenging the status quo. But remember we earlier talked about automating your finances and this is where it comes to play – rather than attempting to make the habit a second nature, simply put it on autopilot – automate your finances.

When it comes to paying yourself first, there is no immediate gratification, but having automatic deposits is an excellent way to start. Also, the amount of money you choose to transfer to your savings account depends on your goals which we have discussed before. Your goal could be to settle your debts if you're indebted, start saving if you don't have debts to settle or invest if you don't have a debt and you're already saving. So, you need to create a budget and automate your finances to help you adhere to the budget you created.

For self-employed

It's often easier for employees who receive their paycheck twice every month or monthly to automate their finances and pay themselves first. But it's a lot harder to save a particular amount of money when you run a business. With the ups and downs of good and bad months, it is not always easy to determine how much you'll earn each month. Is there a way to pay yourself first even when your pay isn't consistent? Yes, that's very possible. What you can do is to set a budget based on an average monthly earning. Consider increasing the amount of money you pay yourself during months you performed better in your business by transferring it to a separate savings account. Now, you can ensure your cash flow remains stable even when you experience a slower month or quarter by withdrawing from the account.

Generally, businesses have cycles and we tend to spend money when we notice an increase in our income, but the "not-so-great" month will definitely come, so how do you manage to meet your needs? Increasing your savings during the good months is the best option in this case.

Some business owners actually pay themselves salary, but this isn't common among many small business owners. However, if you belong to that class, then you can agree on setting aside a specific percentage of your income as an emergency fund. Don't make the mistake of leaving so much of your funds in your business account and leave yourself with very little or nothing at the end of the month. As a business owner, you're no different than everyone else because you still need to look out for yourself too. Having so many responsibilities in your business doesn't imply that you shouldn't set aside some money personally. Remember, you are your own greatest asset, so you have to consider your long-term well-being first before other financial commitments. No one else can save for you – not your brother, friend, parents, employer or spouse but you!

Chapter V

Cutting down your expenses

Shortly after I got married, one of the first lessons we learned was the importance of reducing our monthly expenses, but we learned this lesson the hard way. Of course, as newlyweds with two of us nice-paying jobs, we were quick to get carried away by the desire to buy anything we wanted, whenever we wanted them and any quantity we desired. This included having two new cars, different electronic products and nice things to fill our home. I was still working on my money mindset at the time, so I would once in a while make mistakes.

Well, we also had debts to settle, but things changed after several months when my partner discovered that we were going to have a baby. Well, with the excitement of expecting our baby was also the realization that my wife will have to stay home after our baby is born. This also implies that we will be letting go of one good-paying job and you know what this means – there would be a significant drop in our income with a significant increase in our monthly expenses since we will have an additional mouth to feed. So, this was when it dawned on us that it was time to make extreme changes to our lifestyle and if we fail to do so, then our debt would keep increasing and we may never enjoy the kind of life we desired. It was one of those turning points in life where we had to face reality and make drastic changes. We sat down and discussed how we were going to live off my income and still offset our debt. To achieve our goal, we used a strategy that I used several years ago which helped me to track my spending.

Keeping track of your spending

Have you observed that it's easy for us to just blow through our money without even having an idea of where all our money is going to? But if you truly desire to spend less than you earn, then it's crucial to analyze where and how you spend your money. This will help you to break up with bad financial habits and embrace new ones. One of the best ways to track your income as well as expenses is to have a budget which we will be discussing later.

Other healthy financial habits you need to cultivate include spending less than you earn which we're discussing in this chapter, having some money set aside for emergencies, taking advantage of pretax benefit since less income implies fewer taxes, becoming transparent with your debt, paying your bills on time and automating your savings. I strongly recommend that you create a checklist which could be a piece of paper just like your to-do list. Your goal is to write down your spending for the week, then place it in your wallet along with your cash. Don't forget that one of the smartest ways to reduce your accumulation of debt is to avoid using credit cards and use more of cash.

What you will do with the table is to write down every single cash you use each day as well as the items you bought with the money.

Just keep the entire process as simple as possible to avoid being discouraged. Write down the amount of cash you spent and what you spent the money on which will require a minute or two to complete. As soon as it becomes easy for you, then keep a record of your cash spending each day for a week. Please note that you shouldn't just track your spending only on days that are convenient for you – do it every day. If you do it only when it's convenient, then you'll not have accurate information about your spending and this could cause you to miss a crucial source of careless expenses you often make. You can adopt the envelope strategy by moving your cash to envelopes and tagging each envelope for different purposes. No matter how small your expenses may be (even as low as $5 or 5 cents), you need to record such expenses. Also, whenever you write a check or use your debit or ATM card in making payments, remember to write the amount in your expenses' checkbook. All the information will help you have a complete picture of what you spend over time.

As soon as you have the information about your expenses for a few days, proceed to the next phase which is to combine all your numbers into one document showing your weekly and monthly spending records. Now, having a month's record of your spending is extremely useful because most of your daily and weekly expenses fall into a monthly cycle. You can monitor your weekly spending to enable you have a total amount of money spent at the end of each month by dividing your weeks based on the days of each month. So:

- The first week begins on the first day of the month and it will end on the 7th
- Week 2 begins on the 8th of the month and will end on the 14th
- The third week will also start on the 15th of the month and will end on the 21st
- The fourth and last week will begin on the 22nd of the month and end on the last day of the month. This also implies that the last week will exceed seven days (nine or ten days)

Keeping track of your spending this way means that your "week" may begin and end in the middle of a week. It also implies that the fourth week would exceed the normal number of weeks. But when you monitor your spending for four weeks with this strategy, then you would have succeeded in covering the entire month and also add all your expenses – utilities and housing expenses.

To help you with the entire process, you can make use of the form below and the good thing about the form is that you can easily modify the categories or add categories just to help you group your expenses easily. The first time I began to use this strategy to track my expenses, I added so many categories and ended up making the whole process complicated. This also discouraged me and I abandoned the form as well as the checkbook for recording my daily and weekly spending. After several attempts, I decided to make it as simple as possible and I got amazing results so it wasn't difficult to recommend it to my partner. Your goal is not to complicate the whole process but to have a good idea of your expenses – instead of a microscopic view of all the details.

Monthly Spending	Week 1	Week 2	Week 3	Week 4	Spending Plan
Mortgage or rent					
Water/sewage					
Property tax/association fees					
Electricity					
Heat/fuel					
Telephone - basic					
Home maintenance					
Pet/veterinarian					
2nd mortgage/equity loan					
Groceries/household goods					
Kids' allowance					
Vacation/travel					
Lessons /tuition					
Health club					

Alcohol					
Health & beauty					
Emergency fund					
Drugs /prescriptions					
License/dues					
Gifts /major/other					
Public transportation					
Life insurance (outside of work)					
Cable /videos /DVDs					
Car maintenance					
Vehicle payment/lease					
Gasoline/tolls/parking					
Telephone - long distance					
Trash					
Cellular/pager/Internet					
Meals out/lunches					

Dental/vision expense (out of pocket)					
Child support					
Medical expense (out of pocket)					
Child care					
Laundry/dry cleaning **Clothing**					
Home owner's /renter's insurance					
Contributions/don ations					
Gaming (lottery, casino, etc.)					
Car insurance					
Tobacco					
Entertainment /hobbies					
Other expenses					
Total Expenses					

Monthly Savings from my spending plan:

Learning to spend less than your paycheck

"I have enough money to last me the rest of my life, unless I buy something."

– Jackie Mason

Just before I share some smart ideas on how to cut down on your expenses, let me explain what you need to do with the last column on the far right of the table above *"spending plan."* This column is where you're going to write down your goal for every category of spending (entertainment, food, utilities, etc.) which you'll see shortly. So, at the end of the month, you should have the total amount of money you saved after cutting down on your expenses.

We were ruthless in cutting down on the things we spent money on and I'll be sharing some of the changes that we made in this chapter. Earlier I started our journey to financial education on how to manage our finances by looking at our money mindset. Our mind is the engine house and if it's not in a good shape, then every other thing I'm going to share may not be effective. Now that you've examined your money mindset, go ahead and make the necessary changes in your belief system Once you've done that, then the next thing you need to do is to understand the principles of becoming wealthy in life. *"In simple terms, if you want to be wealthy, then you need to first earn some money, spend less than what you're earning, save as much as you can and invest what you've saved."* Once you complete this cycle, then go ahead and repeat this process. This is what we shall be considering in this book and this chapter will focus more on how to spend less than you earn.

I can guarantee you that even though this process appears to be a simple set of instructions on paper, it's not as simple as it seems when it comes to its implementation. A concept isn't an easy one to practice just because it looks simple. But I'm not also trying to discourage you because, with simple changes you can make in your lifestyle, you can experience lasting and meaningful results as long as you stick to the things you've learned.

So, how can you really spend less than what you and your partner earn? Understanding this financial concept will help you build wealth and if you fail to live less than you earn, then you may never experience financial freedom. When I began to practice some of the concepts I'm about to share with you, I was almost getting discouraged because I wasn't seeing all the results I expected. But with time, I realized that its results take some time to fully manifest. I spent quite a lot of time making the right changes, but the more I did it, the easier the whole process was for me to continue practicing sound financial concepts. Here are the key things you need to do to help you spend less than you earn:

Have a budget

As I mentioned briefly, one of the healthy financial habits you need to cultivate is to have a budget for your family. It's not difficult to make a budget when you know where your money is going. Before you make a budget for your home, you need to be clear about your recurring expenses as well as the amount of money you spend on variable costs which includes travel, groceries, entertainment, gas, internet, etc. I'll be discussing more about budget and how to make one in chapter four. Just bear in mind that your budget is a tool that can help you to control how you spend your money and you can easily free up some cash monthly simply by refining your budget.

Establish an emergency fund

It's easy to conclude that having an emergency fund is not in any way related to how to spend less, but it does. When you have an emergency fund, it helps you to handle unexpected expenses which ensures that you don't spend more money than you earn by using your credit cards or blowing your credit cards. We will be looking at how to build an emergency fund later.

By spending less than what you earn, you will no longer be playing catch up; in fact, living a paycheck-to-paycheck lifestyle would be a thing of the past. Of course, you know that it's often a stressful and paralyzing experience to live paycheck to paycheck, I experienced it before so I can attest to that. But one way to enjoy a quality and stress-free life is to earn more than you spend. You will significantly reduce your money worries and have enough money to save and even invest for your future.

Reduce your expenses

One of my hobbies is bargain hunting and I have learned to save money. Interestingly, saving money is beyond looking for bargains because it could be all about staying away from spending the little you have altogether. For instance, one simple way to save money is to bring your lunch to work rather than embracing the habit of eating out every day. You can save some money by renting things you don't need for the long-term instead of buying them and cluttering your home with items you don't want. Instead of running your air conditioner, you can open your windows as long as the weather isn't too hot for you. Instead of spending over $420 on a new Blu-ray movie, you can stream movies online. You can save money by working from home or even try carpooling to cut costs. The truth is that there are several ways to save money – it all depends on how creative you are.

You need to learn how to cut your expenses in an effective and easy to implement way. This will help to prevent the negative impact of exceeding your monthly budget. I've compiled some smart ways to cut your monthly expenses which will also help you save huge sums of money over time.

Saving on transportation

Undoubtedly, another word for cars is *"money pits."* The reason why some financial experts call cars *"money pits"* is that they are a source of spending from different angles. Apart from the fact that the value of your car is fast depreciating with time, you also spend quite a lot of money purchasing fuel. That's not all; every car will also require various kinds of pricey maintenance. The price of owning a car is high – interests, insurance, maintenance, car payments, gas, parking costs and several others. Have you considered how much you will be saving simply by reducing the cost of automobile in your monthly budget? Well, I almost forgot to mention that the price often doubles when you have more than one car just like I once did.

Back to the story I shared at the beginning of this chapter, once we agreed to cut our expenses, the first place we looked at was the two cars we were having and estimated how much it cost us to maintain the two each month. Finally, we realized that the cost of having two cars was just unnecessary so we decided to sell the one that's more expensive to maintain and retain the other one. Now we made some money from the amount we will be saving which we often spend on car maintenance and also from the sale of the car. Here are smart ways to save money on transportation:

Make use of public transportation. Although it's still unclear how post-COVID-19 would look like, public transportation will always be an excellent option when commuting. It helps you to save a lot of money on gas, maintenance, and parking overtime. Whenever you leave your car behind and commute to work and back, attend important events and visit friends, you're saving money.

With the increase in the number of Rideshare services such as Uber, Lyft, and several others, it's now easier than it has ever been to live without owning a car in major cities around the world. With such services, you can rent or hire a car for occasional trips to the country and other special events. Several months after my wife delivered our son, I decided to let her use the car while I used public transportation to get to work and move around. It's been an exciting experience especially when I decided to check how much I spent on commuting to work for three months – saving over $1000. Another great option is to carpool to work – share a ride to and from work with others. This will help you to save on gas, reduce the wear and tear on your car and offer other benefits. So, I would suggest that you sell your rarely used car to save money on insurance since you're not using it. Also, if you have two or more cars and you're able to maintain them and save, that's great.

But if you're unable to increase your savings and investment while having more than a car, then the best thing to do right now is to sell the other cars and have just one car. You can increase your savings with the proceeds or pay off high-interest debt. One last tip I would love to share with you on how to save on transportation is to always ensure that your car tires are inflated appropriately. Did you know that every two PSI of air added to the tires of your vehicle can result in a significant improvement in your gas mileage by one percent? Always ensure that you check the air pressure in your car tires and you can even take advantage of local gas stations that offer free air and also cut costs.

Smart ways to cut down your energy bills

Depending on where you live, we spend a lot of money on energy bills when we plug all kinds of gadgets during summers and winters. In the United States, for instance, it's estimated that the average home spends around $2,060 annually. Imagine cutting down on this amount by half? Thanks to technology, there are some effective ways to lower the amount of money we spend on energy and improve energy efficiency. What kind of lightbulbs are you using in your home? You need to update your lightbulbs by using CFLs or LED light bulbs in your home. I was amazed to discover that LED light bulbs are actually about four times more energy-efficient than the old incandescent bulbs. In fact, they are not just efficient, but can even last for many years which also saves you the cost of replacing your bulbs several times.

You can make use of the lumens number in comparing the bulbs you want to use and not the equivalent wattages. The reason is that the lumens will reveal the real amount of light that the bulb emits. When you switch all the bulbs in your home, you enjoy cumulative savings in your electric bill at the end of the year.

Are you fond of leaving your lights on when you're not in your room? Doing that will only increase your electricity bill. Whenever you're leaving the room, you can cut your energy bills by turning your lights off. If you have a forgetful partner or kids at home, you can even place helpful reminders and stickers beside the switch.

Another smart way to cut down on your energy usage is to install a programmable thermostat. The benefit of having one in your home is that it will automatically change the cooling and heating of your home even when you're at work, asleep, etc. This ends up saving you good money on your cooling and heating bill. With a programmable thermostat, you can cool or heat your home before arriving from work.

Most of us would rather leave an electrical device plugged in at home even when we're not using them or we rarely use them. Well, most of these devices that remain plugged in will continue to use a small amount of electricity (phantom charge) and this will over time add up especially when you have many devices and small appliances at home. By unplugging various items or power strip that you rarely use, you will eliminate that usage. Consider turning on or turning off electrical devices by using power timers and power strips. When you use a power strip with a switch on it, it helps to block the phantom charges on most of your devices when turned off. Also, the timer helps to automatically turn off the electrical charge that a power strip is receiving as well as the ones received by devices that are plugged into it. This can happen at a specific time of every night based on your usage. When you use smart power strips, they can also help to manage the flow of electricity to certain devices based on a control device. So, if you have a DVD player at home, for instance, it won't receive power until you turn on your television. You can eliminate phantom charges on your electronic devices at home when you're not using them (especially at night) by making use of power strips and power timers.

What about water heater in your home? It's estimated that water heater which is essential for every home especially during winter is a major source of energy drain. In fact, it accounts for about 14 percent of the energy costs of homes. But have you observed that the water in the heater is often hotter than what most of us really need? In addition, most of the heat will end up being lost to the environment which implies that you will be burning extra energy than you should while trying to keep the water hotter than you need. There are smart ways to also save your energy cost here and that's by dropping the temperature to 140°F (about 60°C). To ensure that you retain the heat, you can install a water heater blanket that can pay for itself within one year and thereafter, it will be saving you money monthly. Consider insulating your exposed hot water pipes as well to increase your energy savings. The last tip I would share with you is to air seal your home. When you air seal your home, you will prevent drafts which is a common challenge in older homes. You can significantly increase your utility bills when there is a loss of warm air in the winter and also a loss of cool air in the summer.

Cut down your entertainment costs

Although this is what most people focus on mainly whenever they're attempting to cut costs, they often end up ignoring some regular expenditures that are also gradually eating away at their financial foundation. Shortly after we concluded on selling our second car, the next thing we looked at was entertainment cost and the truth is that it also helped us save cost.

The first cost we had to tackle was our cable bill. I noticed that there were many channels that we never watched for several months but were part of our subscription. So, we looked at the various options available while retaining our favorite shows. Although we downgraded to the basic cable, we ended up eliminating our cable bill later. The reason why we decided to move on was that we found other ways to keep ourselves busy after looking at the implication of staying glued to the TV. Apart from cutting down on our electricity bill, we were no longer exposed to most of the tempting commercials that compel us to buy the things we don't really need at home. This is an excellent way to cut costs and focus on the more important aspects of life. If you're still interested in specific shows, you can use other streaming services such as Hulu+, Netflix and Amazon Prime.

What about your club membership? How much do you spend to be a member of a gym or a local country club? How often do you make use of these services? When was the last time you went to the gym? The truth is that if you're using a country club membership less than once in a month or if you hardly go to the gym, then you're simply throwing your money away. Here's what you can do; suspend your membership of a gym or club for at least one month and see if you genuinely miss them. If you don't, then please save your money and go for a run in the park or walk every evening. Create a home exercise routine and enjoy working out with your partner and kids too. Depending on your fitness goals, investing in exercise equipment may also be an excellent option, but remember, you will be increasing your utility bills. You may be thinking, *"So, if I cancel my club and gym membership, and even downgrade my cable to basic, what other entertainment options do I have?"* Well, are there volunteer groups and organizations in your neighborhood? You may discover that your community offers various options that aren't expensive. For instance, you can attend local community events such as art fairs, music festivals as well as other free entertainment options. Interestingly, any money you save is money you don't need to spend on entertainment – you can increase your savings.

I'm always fascinated by how we easily get seduced by fancy creams that claim to eliminate wrinkles, minimize pores and make our skins healthy. Well, one thing health experts have agreed on is that all that the skin requires is lots of water for hydration and a good diet. Instead of buying expensive creams, consider some cheap options such as almond or coconut oil. Although they are cheap, they can leave your skin looking great too.

Saving money on food

One of the most common problem areas that most people face is food because most of us spend too much money on groceries. We eat too much and even eat out. This ends up causing our waistline to swell, many are obese and we spend so much money on food. If you're serious about cutting costs and saving more, then you need to eliminate waste and save money on food.

Just before I got married, I was always fond of eating out, especially during lunch. As soon as my colleagues go for lunch, I'll join them and I was spending so much on food. My partner wasn't impressed by the fact that I was always eating out while at work. Interestingly, cooking is one of her favorite tasks and you should taste her food – delicious! Whenever I'm done with work for the day, I always look forward to three things; seeing my wife and son and I'm always looking forward to her delicious food. Okay, back to what I was saying, we agreed that she will be packing my lunch for me. I have saved a lot of money by taking my lunch to work. After taking my lunch to work for six months, I realized that I was saving about $100 each month. So, within six months, I had already saved over $600 and $1200 at the end of the year. Whenever you cook at home (which is always a great idea), try to increase the quantity of food you prepare so you can convert the leftovers to lunch and don't forget that there are creative ways to make leftovers as tasty as the original. I don't freeze ready food; I enjoy eating my food fresh. I guess the reason for my love for fresh food is that I like to cook, so I'm always eager to prepare a meal.

Take out as well as dining out is sometimes a huge time saver for most people – especially busy families, however, the cost of eating out is also high. There are smart ways to eat at home conveniently – increasing the quantity of food you prepare and freezing them as I earlier mentioned is one of your options. When cooking, consider simple recipes that require fresh produce in season in your location. Do you have sufficient space in your home for a garden? One of the best hobbies that is also profitable is vegetable gardening. You can concentrate on vegetables that produce abundant fruit and are easy to grow such as tomato. If you have excess, then research various ways to store your excess produce.

When shopping, it's often easy to simply buy what you need without considering larger packages of nonperishables. You may feel that such packages are just too much, but have you ever considered the cost per unit of some of these items? You can get a better deal by looking at the cost per unit of all the different sizes available. What are some of the common nonperishables you often use at home? They include items such as sugar, soap, salt, shampoo, and several others. The cost you save when you buy these items in bulk can add up significantly. You can purchase most of the products (this includes food) in a generic form for a lot less amount of money than the branded ones. Whenever I go shopping, I always look at the ingredients of both branded and generic products to identify how similar they are. Once I discover that they are close, I simply choose the generic one and I can guarantee you that you will still get the same value from non-branded products. This is an excellent way to trim money from your shopping bill consistently. However, I endeavor to test or taste the generic version of the products I purchased twice just to be sure that I like them. Once I discover that I like them and they don't have any unpleasant taste or feel, I'll continue buying them. But be careful because some generic versions have turned out badly, so you still need to try them out.

Saving money on miscellaneous expenses

Are you still interested in other ways to cut down on your monthly expenses? Well, let's dig deeper to find out potential savings in your budget. Have you considered how well you use your smartphone's data plan? If you don't always use it much, then downgrading to a cheaper cell phone plan would be a nice idea. Also, are you making use of all the features you're paying for? Is it possible to drop some of the features with alternatives or the ones you're not using frequently? Saving $10 each month will add up to $120 every year.

Do you spend so much on childcare? We agreed that my wife will have to stay home and take care of our son while I work. Although we were no longer enjoying the added income from her paycheck, we also enjoyed the benefit of not using childcare services. But if you and your partner are working, then you need to pay for childcare. Before settling for one, compare the various childcare options within your area. You may be surprised to find a cheaper alternative that also provides better value. If you happen to live close to your parents then have you considered the possibility that your parents would be willing to watch their grandchildren while you're at work? Go ahead and explore all your alternatives and ensure you're not paying much for childcare. Another important thing I want to mention is the cost of registering your kids for organized child activities. This cost usually gets out of control if you fail to control it. So, find out the real expenses that are associated with each sport before your kids can sign up.

I remember challenging my wife to cut down on her spending on clothes, it wasn't an easy discussion, but I'm glad I talked about it. I discovered that she had just so many clothes that she rarely used and continued to buy more clothes when she gets the chance. Her spending on clothes was so much that when she trimmed her spending in half, the money she saved was much and she has never looked back after the first time she did it. I've always wondered why most people spend so much money on clothes and fail to use most of them. Dressing well for work and other occasions is perfectly okay but you need to be smart about how you buy clothes. It's possible to save plenty simply by buying fewer clothes that are of high-quality so you can utilize the wardrobe you currently have.

Finally, one of the options that many people tend to ignore is moving to a less expensive area. Perhaps one reason for this is the chances of getting a better job in another location. However, checking other areas of your country where you can get another job is worth considering. Find out how much they are willing to accept and compare the housing, you may be surprised at what you will discover when you compare suburban or rural areas with city options.

Chapter VI

Budgeting & financial planning

A good number of people find it hard to maintain a household budget. In fact, many families simply function without having any kind of spending plan while some who believe they have one may not be doing it right. Others see budgeting as merely a kind of tracking tool to help them monitor their expenses. But budgeting is more than just a tracking tool; it's more than taking stock of how you spend your money or recording receipts.

Considering all the demands of maintaining a household, you would agree with me that it's often challenging to find the time to make a budget for your family. It even gets worse when the money left after paying your bills every month is not really significant. I have learned that if we fail to look at our household finances squarely in the eye, then we may not be able to control them; instead, they may end up controlling us. Budgeting is very important for every home, however, learning to establish a household budget requires a lot of effort and it takes time. So, as you read this important chapter, I suggest you grab a cup of coffee, perhaps that will help you focus. Don't forget to also have a pen and paper close by to help you write down your thoughts. Before going into the steps required to set up a family budget, let's have a working definition of a family budget? *"It's simply a record of what you and your partner earn and spend."*

Why do you need to budget your money?

One of the most crucial things you need to do to enable you manage your money is to make a budget. Unfortunately, most people see budgeting as a task for big companies, celebrities, and banks while others are reluctant to embrace this beneficial activity. I believe this is the right time to start learning how to budget your money. You have to stop associating budgeting with a lot of headaches, hassles and restrictions.

Don't feel that the money you have is too small for a budget because if you must manage the small money you earn and even have a life savings, then you have to create a budget. It's one easy way to avoid overspending and make the best use of every single dollar you earn. Here are some reasons why you need to budget your money.

Prevents you from overspending

One of the money personalities out there is the *"big spender"* personality. If you're fond of spending your money without deliberately considering where and what you spend it on, and how much you spend, then you end up overspending every month. Whenever you overspend, you limit your spending power in the future since you will be paying debts with a large chunk of your money. What would life feel like when you only spend most of your income on credit card payments? Of course, this will make it very stressful for you to pay for your daily needs because most of your paycheck have already been channeled to payment of debts. By having a budget, you will be able to determine when you need to stop spending. You can make the process of budgeting easy and simple by making use of various budgeting apps. One of the easiest ways to ensure that you have complete control of your finances is to have a planner for the whole year. While making our New Year resolutions, one of the things we often do is to set our goals for the year. Several studies have confirmed the importance of goal setting and leaders are known to always have a plan. This also applies to your finances; having a 52-week budget planner will serve as your financial guide to help you plan your yearly income and expenses. Remember, if you fail to have a plan, then you're also planning to fail – a weekly budget planner will serve you for a whole year.

When you have a budget planner for the whole year, you will no longer spend money without a purpose. So, I've actually created a 52-week planner that you can use for budget planning and expenses tracking. There is really no better way to monitor your expenses, income and finances than to use a budget planner. In the 52-week planner, you will find different kinds of expenses (fixed, variable and savings) and where to add the amount you spent. Then you will have the cumulative amount of money you spent during the week. At the end of every week, you will have a space where you make your comments regarding the savings you made (after cutting down your expenses or increasing your income) or money spent due to an emergency. This is an excellent way to have a clear picture of what you did with your money every week and this covers the 52 weeks that make up a year. So, if you would like to have one, it's available at Amazon (Title: *How To Manage Money 52-Week Budget Planner*, ASIN: B08B7B2WGK):

Amazon US: www.amazon.com/dp/B08B7B2WGK
Amazon UK: www.amazon.co.uk/dp/B08B7B2WGK

Budgeting helps you to worry less and save money

Generally, individuals who don't have a budget often save less than those who do. The reason is that whenever you create a budget, what you're doing is to assign your funds to specific things based on their level of importance – prioritize. It's possible for you to automatically transfer money into your investment or savings account monthly and you can achieve this through budgeting. Since you have a plan for spending money in a month, you also reduce the chances of touching your savings. This will gradually help you to build wealth and experience real financial freedom.

Another benefit of budgeting is that it helps you to make decisions on how you intend to spend your money on different aspects of your life. So, as a *"saver,"* if you desire to spend a reasonable amount of your money on leisure activities, you wouldn't feel bad about the money you spend as long as you're adhering to your budget, meeting your saving goals as well as other needs. The truth is that some people feel that budgeting limits the fun in their life but that's not true. Based on my experience, one of the things it has helped me to enjoy is that it actually opens up opportunities to have more fun and it helps me worry less about the future. When companies are thinking of laying off staff, I don't feel scared at all because I have sufficient savings that can carry me and my family for several months until I'm able to find a better job. This is one of the greatest benefits of budgeting – it saves you from worrying about your future. It helps you understand clearly what you're going to spend on each category, so you no longer have to be anxious about future expenses.

Makes you more flexible and in control

Budgeting doesn't make you rigid in your spending; it can actually be flexible since you're free to move money from one category to another all through the month. Well, it's also crucial to point out that you should as much as possible avoid touching the money you already set aside as your savings. What you should focus on more is the amount of money you spend on each category. This is also one of the best ways to prevent yourself from overspending and it helps you to recognize pressing issues that need to be addressed. When you have a budget, you can also handle unexpected expenses as they occur in your home. Life is usually difficult and stressful when you're not in control, but when you have a budget, then you will have a feeling of control over your money. This is because it helps you to prioritize your spending, monitor how you're doing and know when you need to stop spending. I remember when I wanted to go on vacation four years ago, I knew it was something that required lots of funds, so I had to budget for it by setting aside a specific amount of money for the trip every month until I saved enough money. But here is the good thing about budgeting and saving; while on vacation, I enjoyed so many facilities that those regarded as *"wealthy"* enjoyed. If I had used my credit card for the vacation, I would have accumulated debts that would affect other aspects of my life. So, budgeting enabled me to plan my life and enjoy what appears to be too expensive for my level of income. It helps you to create a solid plan that you can easily follow as you plan for the future. In fact, in my opinion, budgeting is one of the greatest tools you need to transform your financial future and make the desired changes in your life starting from today. Finally, budgeting doesn't have to be complicated as you will soon discover.

Types of family budget

As soon as you understand how to set up a family budget, it's also crucial to determine the kind of budget you need. Most people feel that there is just one type of family budget and I was in that position before. But with time, I discovered that there are other types of budgets that help families to achieve their collective financial goals. Take a look at some types of a family budget.

1. Survival Budget

While growing up, we often faced tough times and I remember some of the things that happened thereafter. For instance, my dad would explain that we had to live without some of the utilities we enjoyed as he struggled to raise the money for our upkeep. During the times we were living paycheck to paycheck, the kind of budget we used is known as a survival budget. Although we didn't really create a budget or call it a name, it was exactly what we used back then and it worked. At this point, savings and debt repayment are secondary because all that we had was what my dad and mom had with them. Once my dad's wallet is dry, then we will have to wait for the next payday to get relief. I must confess that a survival budget is not fun at all; it is purely a means to survive but it always gets the job done and keeps you going until you're back on your feet.

2. Debt-Free Budget/Comprehensive Budget

At this point, you're no longer concerned about survival because you now have more breathing room. When you use a debt-free budget, then you are free to assert more control over your funds. This is the point where you can start planning for the future without being bothered about when the next paycheck will come. You're more focused on getting out of debt that was accumulated during the survival period and the best way to do this as I've earlier mentioned is to spend less than what you earn.

This is the perfect budget for homes that have limited income and are trying to cut down on their expenses. The budget consists of lists of expenses with categories as well as exact numbers spent each month. It provides all the information that is required to help cut down family expenses in an organized form. It can also serve as an overall budget that is used for reviewing your spending over an extended period.

3. Planning Budget (Often helps those who want to achieve their financial goals)

For those planning their budget based on a specific time of their life or an event, the planning budget will help. The budget type provides a special category in your original family budget to help you plan for specific needs or goals. Also, it makes provision for a column that helps a family to plan for emergency savings as well as life savings.

4. **Problem-Solving Budget (Specifically meant for creating financial safety for homes that are on a budget)**

Although it shares a lot of similarities with the comprehensive budget, this kind of budget is highly recommended when you discover that you're a spender and you are finding it very hard to cut down on your spending in a particular area. What you can do is create a more detailed list that would help you identify specific areas where your money is going as well as those areas you can stop spending on. It's the type of budget that helps to identify problem spending areas in your family budget and how to clearly fix them.

So, how do you know the right type of budget to use? This often depends on what you're trying to achieve and your financial level. You can carry out a financial self-assessment to determine the true state of your finances as well as your goals. For instance, if things are extremely difficult for your family and you're living paycheck to paycheck, then a budget type like the survival budget would be the best option. If you're still in debt and you need to get rid of your debts, then choosing the Debt-free or comprehensive budget would be the best. For those who don't have debts and are looking forward to handling major projects, then the best option would be planning budget.

Steps to budgeting

Remember, the goal of this book is to help you manage your finances effectively – whether you're earning well or your paycheck is small. The basic rule to budgeting is to spend less money than you earn and which we have already discussed in chapter three. When it comes to budgeting, there are six essential steps you need to take.

Step one: meeting with your partner

You don't really need this step if you're alone, but if you have a partner, then it's crucial to ensure that both partners are on the same page. A budget will never work when adults in the family are not on the same page. It's very important to have a heart-to-heart discussion with all decision-makers in your home to look at both individual and shared financial goals. The truth is that every stakeholder in the family will have their priority, but you all will also need to compromise to ensure that you create the budget that's supported by all members of your home.

Step two: select your budgeting tools - electronic or paper

As soon as you're on the same page with other stakeholders in your family, the next thing is to choose your budgeting tool which could either be electronic or paper. This will help you to keep track of your family finances. Although making use of a budget worksheet with a paper and pen can provide you with results that are as accurate as electronic budgeting tools, you can also reduce the number of possible errors by using financial software or electronic budgeting tools. They help to make the entire process easier for you, especially when you're always busy with work and other tasks. But if paper feels right for you, then consider an accounting ledger which doesn't really cost much. They are mainly created for credits and debits within your bank statements. Credits simply imply incoming dollars while debits have to do with all the dollars you're spending. When you make use of a budget tracker, for instance, it can help to create running totals, highlight discretionary spending, track your fixed expenses, makes suggestions, and generally show you how your credit and debit influence each other for your bottom line.

Step three: monitor income and expenses

When writing a budget for your family, another crucial step is to understand your current financial situation. Well, perhaps what's most painful and critical in this whole process is having to face your numbers. You can only create a realistic budget that's based on prioritizing needs, goals as well as wants when you have an idea of how you and your partner spend money. Interestingly, technology has made this process less arduous by doing most of the work for us. This is where the budgeting tool you've chosen comes to play. Well, as I earlier mentioned, you can also do this manually if that's comfortable for you and you have all the time in the world. You also need any document that can show all your incoming and outgoing money (credit and debit) like receipts, bills and credit card statements, statements from all the sources of income, student loan interest and several others. This is where you need to understand the different kinds of expenses you make in your home. Don't forget to use the checklist I suggested where you record your cash expenses every week. This is an excellent way to get accurate data on your expenses.

Basically, there are three categories that will make up your budget and they are the fixed expenses, variable expenses and savings expenses. When learning how to effectively manage your finances, you need to understand the three categories well. They will guide you on how to put your plan into action when creating a budget.

Fixed expenses

This refers to all your expenses that remain the same from time to time. Although the amount you pay may vary a bit for things like utilities, such bills are always due regularly. Some examples of fixed expenses which you can include in your family budget include:

- Lease/car loan repayment
- Property taxes (if you're paying it monthly)
- Debt payments based on your debt repayment plan
- Vehicle insurance (if you pay it monthly)
- Strata fee/condo fee
- Mortgage(s)
- Life/Disability/Extended health insurance

- House/tenant insurance
- Utility bills (electricity, internet, gas, water, cable, cell, etc.)
- Vehicle insurance (if you pay it monthly)
- Rent
- School fees
- Taxes

Since these expenses stay the same and you pay them regularly, they are easy to budget. Even though the bills remain consistent each month, it's possible to lower their costs too. So, you may have the option of choosing an alternative plan with a lower price if you're signed up for a monthly service that you don't use very often.

You can consider shopping around for alternative health insurance, car or life insurance to help you save more money. When you reduce your fixed expenses, you're also increasing the amount of money you save every month. Have you observed that some of the items on the fixed expenses list take up the biggest percentage of your budget? By lowering how much you allocate to fixed expenses, you're also lowering the percentage of your entire budget that is devoted to them. This is a smart way to cut down on your expenses without affecting other spending decisions you make such as buying new clothes, eating out, etc. I can guarantee you that the little amount of money you save on your fixed expenses will always add up fast.

Consider this scenario; back in 2012, I was spending $1200 monthly on rent. While going through my expenses, I decided that I needed to change my apartment and possibly cut down my expenses. So, I set out to get a new apartment and within a week, I agreed on one and the interesting thing is that the quality of the new neighborhood and apartment didn't change much. But at the end of the day, I was able to pay $1100 instead of $1200 and realized a savings of $100. The interesting thing is that $100 each month will turn into $1200 at the end of a year. All I did was just make a smart money-saving decision just once and was able to save for other things.

Savings expenses

This category covers the amount of money you want to save as well as what you want to save for. To save, you just have to identify the purpose of your savings and automate the entire process. The savings expenses category is further divided into two groups – irregular expenses and oriented savings. The irregular expenses refer to some of the costs that appear all through the year and you need to budget for such expenses to avoid using your credit card or other kinds of debts when such expenses come up. Another name for irregular expenses is *"planned spending"* and this covers expenses such as vet bills, health expenses, clothing and shoes (if you go shopping once or twice each year), and gifts. The second category is the goal-oriented savings and you can also include them in your budget. While creating my budget, I always add my vacation savings to this category. If you have a plan to save for a down payment on a home, retirement, a vacation, education, as well as your emergencies, then you can add them to this category. You need to first determine the amount you need to save and when you intend to save it, then divide by the number of months remaining until the date. This will help you determine how much you will set aside monthly.

Variable expenses

I like to define variable expenses as all expenses that fall within your control. So, you have the freedom to determine how much you want to spend on such items. Examples of some items you need to add to this category include:

- Clothing and shoes
- Fuel/public transportation costs
- Lottery
- Personal care items
- Work lunches and snacks
- Babysitting
- Entertainment
- Daycare
- Parking
- Alcohol/tobacco
- Sports, recreations and your hobbies
- Eating out
- Medical and dental fees
- School expenses such as stationery and textbooks
- Groceries
- Children's lessons and activities
- Haircare and salon services
- Home maintenance and household items
- Magazines/books/newspapers

It may be harder to cut back on variable expenses than fixed expenses since most of the expenses in this category significantly affect your lifestyle. You need a lot of *"day-to-day willpower"* to cut back on variable expenses than fixed expenses.

Once you have divided them into three groups: debit, savings and credit, you also need to come up with the total of each group in your budget. You may discover that your outgoing is more than your incoming and this sometimes makes the process scary. Well, it shouldn't be scary because the entire budgeting process will help you to correct this soon.

Step four: your current situation

While tracking your expenses, it's crucial to place them in different categories that you can easily understand. So, create categories like debt payments, housing, entertainment and dining out. During this exercise, you will discover interesting things about how you spend your money. For me, I was amazed at how much I spend dining out every month. It was one of the things that I resolved that I was going to remove from my list of expenses. Although I love giving my wife a treat, I agreed that what I was spending was too much, but I can still dine out with my wife – just not as many times as I was doing before. As soon as you know how much you spent in every category, then you have to also determine the expenses that change and the ones that are fixed all through the year. It's always an excellent idea to identify the discretionary categories – these are things that you spend money on but are nonessentials for your home. I would advise that you pause here and grab a pen and paper as I earlier suggested. Call for a meeting with your partner and go through the steps I already shared with you. What are the categories you're spending excessively? I already shared my experience where I quickly identified that I was spending so much on food because I was dining out frequently. You need to identify areas that are nonessential where you spend a lot of money; it could be on electronics, entertainment, food, travel, etc.

Step five: now set up your budget software, spreadsheet or ledger

Once you've learned how to create a budget for your family and you now have the total figures, the next thing is to take all the initial totals for every category and add them to your budget software, ledger or spreadsheet. If you're doing this, then you will notice that the budget is beginning to take shape now. At this point, your short-term goal is simple – make sure that your expenses (debits) are less than your income (credits). This brings us to the next step which involves controlling your discretionary spending.

Step six: cut costs

You just have to trim costs just as I did. What are the categories you're spending too much money on? Are you currently unable to save some money or pay your debts? If your answer is yes, then you need to trim expenses right away. The truth is that every one of us will have items on our budget that we can cut without feeling it. For instance, by simply buying things in bulk, you can cut down how much you spend on groceries and you can reduce the number of times you eat out and eat more at home. You can even make your lunch instead of spending more money eating out with friends and colleagues.

One of the best ways to manage discretionary spending is to automate your finances based on the information you got from your budgeting process. Later in chapter six, I'll be sharing various ways to automate your finances and ensure that you stick to what you've created in your budget. If you decided to cut the number of times you dine out in your budget, then you also need to reduce the total amount of money you spend on food to reflect the change. When you automate the process, then you know how much you have to spend until the next payday and this helps you manage your finances better.

Experts recommend keeping both food and housing cost under a third of your income. The goal here is to ensure that you have enough money left over to cover your savings and common expenses. Also, while creating your spending plan, consider using this category break down to assist you:

- Food (both home and away) 15-30 percent
- Savings 10-15 percent
- Clothing 3-10 percent
- Housing (mortgage or rent) 20-35 percent
- Family necessities (hair care, toiletries, laundry, etc.) 2-4 percent
- Utilities (water, gas, telephone, electric, trash, etc.) 4-7 percent
- Transportation (gas, repairs, bus fare, car payment, insurance) 6-30 percent
- Medical (bills, prescription and insurance) 3-8 percent
- Entertainment 2-6 percent

Remember to always review your credit card as well as your statements to always remind you of how you're spending your money. It's not always a smart idea to spend all your cash-on-hand on bills. It's better to spread out your bills evenly over the month.

Managing a budget surplus or deficit

It's possible to have a budget deficit after developing your budget. This is where you're unable to assign enough funds to all your needs. The best way to avoid having a budget deficit is to cut down on your expenses. Also, if you underestimated your income or overstated any of your expenses, you may have a deficit. If you didn't underestimate your income or overstate your expenses, you may need to reevaluate your desired standard of living for your family. Consider lowering them to avoid increasing your debt. Another option you have is to create other sources of income to help cover the deficit and even if your added source of income provides you with more money than you needed to offset the deficit, then there are many things you can do with the surplus. Some of the tips which I'll be sharing with you later will help.

Once you get rid of things you don't really need you should be able to resolve the deficit. But what I always look forward to whenever I'm developing my budget is a budget surplus. What this implies is that after writing down the amount I need to spend for each category, I still have more money left which I'm yet to assign to anything. So, what do you do when you find yourself in such a situation?

The first thing I always do which I also encourage you to do is to crosscheck your budget. Did you overestimate your income or underestimate some of your expenses? Take some time to check every item on your budget and if all is okay, then there are many options available. If you have debts to pay, then apply the surplus to the payment of debts. If you don't have any debt, then you can increase your emergency funds or retirement fund.

Undoubtedly, managing your finances is both complex and simple, however, the moment you understand the steps to creating a family budget, you will have complete control of your finances. It's all about understanding your family income (which could be the combination of what you and your partner earn within a specific period), how much you owe as well as what you spent over a specific period. The hard part involves choosing where to cut back after reviewing your spending and how to divert or allocate more money.

How do you motivate yourself to stick to your budget? For some people, especially savers, watching their savings account as it grows is enough motivation, but others may require some creative ways to stick to their budget. If you fall into this category, you can set goals for your money. What are the things that would make you feel great financially? Go ahead and identify a secondary goal and work toward it. While developing my budget, I always set a goal for myself, it could be a vacation which I normally do. There is nothing more motivating as saving for a fancy vacation and you can even achieve this by using a budget surplus. Once you come up with goals that can motivate you, write them down on a piece of paper and stick it to your fridge or any place you can easily see them daily. Make it more fun by involving every member of your family in writing down the goals. Once you all have agreed on the best options, you will discover that the goal will motivate everyone to work toward achieving it. But if you're the only one setting the budget goal, your spouse may continue to spend while you struggle to meet up with your savings.

Chapter VII

Get out of debt & stay debt-free

Understanding the emotional side of saving and spending

While growing up, one of the commonest things I hear people say is that it's importance to have a life saving to help handle financial setbacks such as a sudden illness that either requires a lot of money to treat or reduces income, loss of a job, or an injury. I even tried saving while I was a teenager but it wasn't easy at all, especially while living with a father who is a big spender. As soon as I saved enough money, I would become tempted to spend part of it on something I like. This is common among most people; a good number of people are aware of the need to build up our savings for our children's education, our retirement, or even a down payment for a home. Everyone agrees that increasing the amount of money we save while reducing our debts is the best thing to do, but the rate of savings is significantly shrinking while there is also an increase in the level of personal debt.

So why do we always behave in self-destructive and irrational ways when it comes to matters relating to money? Why did I withdraw money from my savings just to pay for something I like – which I didn't really need? Part of the answer is that humans are no not very rational and we're no calculating machines. Humans have complex emotional needs and the way we manage our money and credit affects our emotions in very different ways that are difficult to control. We're often faced with the tension of *"later"* and *"now"* every day. Although there is so much *"immediate"* pleasure in spending, we often experience the pain of paying our debt later. Also, we don't always enjoy the benefits of saving immediately. Just as I experienced while growing up, most of us (even though we see ourselves as mature adults) still have so much of a two-year-old in us. It's easy for *"I want it now"* to suppress *"but think about **later**."* How we deal with our finances is undoubtedly tied to our experiences while growing up.

The thing about debt is that it has a *"snowball effect"* which makes things difficult. The first reason why you accumulate debt is that you lack money to settle a specific need. This debt further increases how much you spend for several months and years to come. This also means that the likelihood of you borrowing money again (possibly more than you've borrowed before) to settle your future expenses will increase significantly. Although you may pay your bills and purchase the things you need with debt just to solve your immediate needs, it only increases the size of the problem you'll have to deal with down the road. The moment this debt cycle starts, it will require a lot of work and commitment on your part to turn this cycle around. Debt also affects our emotional well-being because when your debt keeps increasing instead of decreasing, then you may feel desperate, trapped and even lose control of your life. It leaves you with the feeling that someone else now "owns" you and you would no longer give yourself the breaks as well as pleasures you need to make life interesting and keep you healthy and happy. When you're having so much debt to pay, it could drain your sense of self-worth and confidence. This will result in depression, anxiety and other unhealthy issues in your life. The emotional side effects of a debt problem can also affect your relationship with friends, children, extended family and can even damage your marriage.

Did you know that the single biggest factor that leads to problems in relationships (which even ends in divorce) is money issue? It cuts across all aspects of your life and can significantly affect your performance at work because you may end up forcing yourself to overwork. When you overwork, you also expend your energy and lose the creativity that can add value to your employer which could lead to promotions, bonuses and raises.

Now you know why debt is a two-edged sword which if used carefully and wisely will lead to prosperity and if used without proper planning will cause economic crisis in addition to the emotional stress associated with it.

Why you accumulate debt

The best way to start is to first examine the reasons why you accumulate debt because if you fail to address the source of the problem, then you will always have debt issues. Sometimes, we accumulate debt just to pay for unforeseen emergencies or due to the loss of a job.

However, the commonest reason why people accumulate debt has to do with poor spending habits.

It always costs you more money to spend money, unless you're spending cash. Just see the credit card as someone granting you a favor by allowing you to purchase something you can't afford presently, but can pay off in the future. The implication is that you will keep owing more money and *"own less."* For almost 100 years now, we have been talking about the Joneses – our dear neighbors who have the kind of life and stuff we desire – but we haven't been able to keep up with them. You will always accumulate large amounts of debt when you're never contented with what you have. You will further increase your credit card balances or keep them static when you lack the knowledge required to manage debt and get out of debt forever. Here is a good example of why you always accumulate debt: imagine purchasing an item for $500 and justify your purchase by looking at the amount you will be paying each month. So, you simply conclude that it's manageable to make $15 payments each month. However, it's often hard to notice that the lender is right there expecting interest charges of about $147 which will be added to the $500. Of course, in four years, you offset the $500 which you paid at a specific interest rate of 14.7 percent. Well, a good number of credit cards actually have higher interest rates for the $500 purchase you made. For instance, an interest rate of 22 percent will imply that you will end up paying extra $280 to the credit card company. Guess what? You will have enough time to pay the $780 but what will be the worth of the item (after four years) when you finally own it? But that's not all, when you finally add the larger investments of our lives such as weddings, college costs, unplanned medical emergencies, financed homes, relocation, unemployment, and several others and you will fully understand why it's always easy for debt to accumulate with time. When you spend more than what you're earning, then you will undoubtedly live a debt-centered financial life. The solution to spending more than what you earn is in developing a budget to help guide you as you spend your money.

The main reason why most people accumulate debt is one or a combination of most of the factors we've just discussed and once you can clearly identify the reasons why you go into debt; you can stop it from happening again. If you don't have a straightforward plan to offset what you owe, you will continue to increase your debt via interest.

How do you know you have too much debt

Do you always think of credit as cash instead of debt? Are you a compulsive or impulsive spender? If your answer is yes to any of these questions, then it's a sign that you may experience financial challenges soon. You're likely going to accumulate debt if you don't know how much you're owing or your monthly living expenses.

You're headed for financial trouble if you're owing more than seven creditors or your debts are more than your assets. If you and your spouse are not honest with each other regarding the use of credit, then your debt may grow. When you depend on extra income such as overtime by your spouse to assist you in meeting your basic needs, then you're undoubtedly headed for financial challenges. Other signs that you may be in debt include when you commit 20 percent of your paycheck to the settlement of credit payments apart from your home mortgage or when you're not paying your rent or utilities on time. If you take out a loan, withdraw money from your emergency funds, skip payments or billed for payments because you can't make credit payments or settle your regular living expenses, then you are likely in a financial mess.

If you discover that four or more of these descriptions apply to you, then it's clear that you need to take a second look at your spending plan. However, if five or more of these descriptions apply to you, then you are definitely headed for financial trouble. But, if seven or more of them apply to you, then you're already in financial danger.

Get out of debt and gain financial freedom

The fact that you've read this book to this point is an indication that you're interested in managing your finances effectively. If you're in debt, then gaining your freedom from debt is a great step toward achieving your goal, and the steps which I will be sharing with your will help you regain control of your finances and cut down on your debt significantly.

You have to admit that you're having a debt problem and the only person in this world who can deal with it is YOU! But you can only solve the problem if you agree that the issue is worth resolving. I suggest you write a statement accepting full responsibility for causing the debt problem and make a commitment to resolve it. Another effective way to make this commitment is to have a family meeting where you openly discuss the debt problems you're having. It's usually rare for one person to solve a debt problem because the suggestions of other members of your family may help you resolve it. This open acknowledgment of having a debt issue brings great relief to others in your home.

Refrain from debt spending

Can you recall the last time you didn't use your credit card throughout an entire day? You need to remove your gas cards, store cards as well as credit cards out of your wallet right now. Keep them somewhere secure and completely out of sight. Instead of using your credit card, consider other options such as a debit card, checks or even cash. This will help to cut down on your spending and help you make planned purchases. Since you can use your debit card the same way as your credit card, having one is an excellent alternative because you can use it as a credit card while avoiding the debit effect of a credit card. The next thing you need to do is to be clear about the number of people you owe as well as how much you're owing each creditor. Fetch your credit statements right away and write down the information about who you owe and how much you owe. You can complete this exercise by using the worksheet below. Add the details of the company you're owing which includes phone number, address and the name of a collection agency or attorney if it has been turned over to an attorney.

Records of debt owed

Company Name	

Account Number	
Address & Phone number	
Priority	
Original Monthly payment	
Is debt secured? If so, by what?	
Has legal action been taken?	
Has legal action been taken?	
Total Balance Owed	
Payment due Date	
Number of payments left	
Amount last paid	
Date last paid	

Add your account number and how much you owe. The next step is to prioritize your debts – which ones are you paying? The reason why you need to determine a priority for settling your debts is that you may not have sufficient funds to settle all your debts. So, settle your debts based on what is going to happen next if you fail to pay them. Do you have a loan with a *"secured"* status? When you secure a loan by collateral, then you need to settle that loan first before others. This is because you may end up losing your property when you fail to pay the loan. When you obtain a secured loan, you pledge your assets or cosign with someone else. On the other hand, when you acquire a loan because of your excellent credit rating then it's an unsecured loan. Also, you have to consider possible legal actions that could be taken, for instance, if you purchased a car and stand the risk of losing it when it's repossessed, you may consider paying the debt as quickly as possible.

Another factor you have to consider is the interest you're paying on the loan – how much are you paying? You can settle the debts with the highest interest rates because they will cost you more over time. What will happen if you're unable to pay the bill on time?

- Will your creditor harass you?
- Do you have a *"grace period'* for settling the debt before a creditor begins to take action toward collecting the money?
- Are you going to lose access to utilities or will you be evicted from your home?
- What if you took a loan from a family member; will this lead to hard feelings?

The best way to approach the settlement of your debts, especially when your funds are insufficient to settle each debt, is to determine what will happen when you fail to pay.

How much are you capable of paying back?

Shortly after listing the details of those you owe, the next thing you need to do is to determine how much you intend to pay every single creditor on your list. Also, it's crucial to know how long it's going to take you to pay back each debt. But what happens when your monthly payments exceed what you're capable of paying from your paycheck? It's always recommended that you settle your debts with 10-20 percent of your paycheck. So, if you're monthly paycheck is $3,500, then you can set aside $350 for settling your debts. However, as I earlier mentioned, you may have numerous debts and this makes it difficult to attend to all your debts. One available option is to find out how to apportion 25 percent of your paycheck to the settlement of your loans. There are several ways to find money to help you settle your loans, especially when you're owing more than what you can pay back each month. The first option is to examine your current living expenses and we have already covered this when we discussed budgeting. So, find out where your funds are going and how to cut down on your expenses. This should leave you with extra funds to settle your loan.

Another thing you can do is to leverage the money in your savings account or money market fund to help settle your debts. You can sell properties that you don't really need such as jewelry, stocks, furniture, car and others to reduce your debt payments. An excellent way to settle your debt is to increase your family income. It will be easier for you to maintain your current lifestyle while repaying your debts when you have an extra paycheck. But it can't prevent you from incurring more debts because it's not a solution to poor money management habits. Getting out of debt will require a combination of good money management habits and effective strategies for paying the debt. Are you the breadwinner of your home? You can add extra dollars to your budget by taking a second job or working extra hours, especially during financial crisis. You can encourage other members of your family to get a job to increase your income. It's possible to increase your income by developing personal skills and talents and earn money with it.

Develop a plan to settle your debts

Now that you're here, I'm convinced that you know how much you owe and how much you can manage to pay back as well as when you will be paying back the debt. You need to move on to the next step which is to choose how much you're going to pay each creditor as well as how long it's going to take to settle each creditor. This is where you would be needing a debt-paying plan to help you settle your creditors within the next three years. Your actual debt payment plan can come in different forms:

- You can choose to pay each creditor an equal amount of money.
- Another option is to increase the amount of money you pay to creditors that you owe the most while you pay smaller amounts to creditors you don't owe much.

- You can also choose to pay each creditor based on the action they might take if you fail to settle your debt in line with your original agreement.

Of course, no creditor will know how much you're paying other creditors because what you're paying is confidential. I must encourage you to pay everyone you owe; however, when you're in a position where the fund you have is insufficient to pay back all your creditors, then you need to carefully decide which bills you need to pay back first.

To help you set up your debt payment plan, I've come up with a worksheet that you can print and adjust as required. In the worksheet, add the details of your creditor's name, the percent of the total amount you owe every single creditor, the amount of the original payment you make each month, and how you want to pay each creditor – equal amounts or based on what may likely happen. Remember to write down precisely how much you're paying each creditor every month and once the creditor accepts your plan, then you can put down the real amount you intend paying each creditor.

Debt payment plan

Company/Individuals Owed							
% of Total Debt							
Original Monthly payment							
Monthly Amount to pay							
December							
November							
October							
September							
August							
July							
June							
May							
April							
March							
February							
January							

Once you have created a plan for paying your debts, go ahead and discuss your new plan with all your creditors. Stop using all your credit cards and desist from taking new loans except you're faced with an extreme emergency. Being in debt is a stressful experience, but avoiding your creditors may likely increase your stress level. This is because they may see you as someone attempting to avoid the payment of debts. So, don't avoid them; instead, pay them a visit and in case you're unable to visit them, then write them and ensure that you communicate with them frequently. Please note that if you're not prepared to repay the debt, then don't send an email. Most creditors would gladly receive a small payment than nothing. Also, it's crucial to note that creditors would prefer to have money instead of the item you purchased with the loan. When communicating with your creditors, inform them that you presently lack the money to make the minimum payment specified on the terms and conditions of the loan. It's equally important to explain the reason why you failed to meet up with your payment such as insurance premiums, death in the family, rising taxes, bad money management skills, divorce, or layoffs. Also, inform them of your current income as well as other obligations. Then proceed to the most important aspect which is where you inform them of how you hope to meet up with your payment and precisely how much you can pay every month.

Now, once you have come up with a plan, you must endeavor to adhere to the plan until you settle all your debts. Make sure you show the creditor a reasonable plan for settling your loans and it's actually possible to convince them to reduce the interest charges, especially in desperate cases. Your debt repayment plan needs to be acceptable by you as well as your creditor. You will end up jeopardizing your chances of getting future credit when you're unable to stick to your proposed plan. You may have to think about loan consolidation or even bankruptcy if you owe a large amount of money and your creditors are not prepared to accept reduced payments.

Chapter VIII

Surviving a recession

During the 2008 recession, I somehow managed to stay employed, however, most of the people I know weren't so lucky because they were either underemployed, furloughed or unemployed at one point. But before I got employed, I struggled to get a good job and during this time, I learned a lot about surviving without a reasonable source of income. Getting just "any job" is not always a good experience because I was turned down several times and failed to get interviewed for jobs I knew I was qualified to do.

The most painful aspect of being unemployed is being in debt. After my experience of not getting a good job and struggling with debts since my pay wasn't enough to sustain me, I concluded that being unemployed and in debt is perhaps the worst thing that can ever happen to anybody. Interestingly, this was what really gave me the kick in the pants to do all I can to get rid of debts and have a decent emergency basket. Although it took me several years after the recession to clear my debts, I haven't looked back again and I'm going to share my experience along with some of the information I got from research. The truth is that the COVID-19 pandemic has caused major industries and businesses around the world to shut down. So here is the big question, are you *"recession-ready"* right now? Before I continue, it's crucial to understand what constitutes a recession.

According to economists, a recession is regarded as two consecutive quarters of economic contraction or negative growth. When most economies around the world have been shut down for several weeks and even more than a month in some countries, then a recession is inevitable. In the United States, the number of unemployment claims has spiked over the past few weeks. But if we're going to experience a recession, how bad will it be and what would be the duration? Unfortunately, I don't have any idea how bad or how long the recession would last – it could be a long and painful recession with a slow recovery or a short one with a quick recovery. Whenever there is a recession, there are several things that are bound to happen. Understanding how it will impact families will help you know the right steps to take to protect your finances. Let's examine some of the possible impacts of a recession on homes and various ways to manage them.

Increase in layoffs and unemployment

The stability of homes as well as individuals is significantly affected by job loss. Losing a job can have a serious impact on our health, well-being, status and self-worth. Although a good number of people who lose their job go ahead and increase their knowledge and explore, many are unable to compose themselves during such times. They end up suffering depression and live in denial.

Being unable to find a job leads to the lack of money to pay bills every month and being a parent means that you have to take care of yourself as well as your partner and kids. So, how can you overcome a possible job loss? This depends on what's obtained in your country. For instance, if you're in the United States, then the first thing you need to do is to file an unemployment claim and we've currently seen a spike in the number of unemployment claims since the outbreak of COVID-19 pandemic. Another option is to borrow money from family and friends and possibly take a lower-paying job. These are all short-term solutions. But long-term solutions would be to work closely with hiring managers to help you find higher-paying jobs. Depending on your finances, you can go back to school while you're still unemployed. This might require you to relocate to a different city. I would suggest that rather than wait for the perfect job that's suitable for your qualification, go for a part-time job to help with money needed to take care of your family while waiting for recruiters to help you find the perfect career for you. You may also want to use this opportunity to change your career, but you need to choose your career path wisely based on global trends.

Finally, you shouldn't see relocating as a last resort because you can increase your chances of getting a new job by simply relocating. Remember to make your resume stand out from the competition before applying for the next job. You may still retain your job, but during a recession, job security is often out of your hands because you may be out of job the moment the company you work for goes out of business. But Some companies may not completely lay off all their employees, so one way to maintain your job in such situations is to become indispensable at work. Becoming indispensable at work implies that you're conscious of the fact that employers don't just hire and pay employees for their time, but most importantly for the value they offer. So, ask yourself, what's the value you offer where you're currently working? If you fail to provide any meaningful value to your employer, then why would they pay you? Right now, I would suggest that you start by identifying the value you're adding to the company you work for – increase in revenue, helping your employer to cut cost, rendering exceptional customer service, etc.

Once you have identified the value you're adding to your employer, think of other ways to increase the value you're bringing to the table and don't forget that there are excellent opportunities to add value to your organization each day, so you have to identify such opportunities and take advantage of them. You will become more indispensable with the more value you can provide. Now, it's impossible to control what takes place in the economy as well as the market, but you still have an area of influence. There is one variable that you can control and that's the level of value you provide your employer so make good use of it. But what happens if you still lose your job despite adding exceptional value to your organization? It's crucial to point out here that the response by different governments to this recession is significantly different than what we experienced during the last financial crisis which took place back in 2008-2009. Perhaps the reason is that the cause of this recession is entirely different and therefore demands a different approach. While the 2008-2009 crisis happened because the banks were at the risk of bankruptcy, this recession is purely as a result of the shutdown of most businesses to prevent the spread of COVID-19. This implies that the banks are still in a strong position, but those who may feel the impact of this recession are businesses and workers. This also explains why the governments in different countries around the world are coming up with various stimulus packages that are aimed at employees and business owners. So, I believe that one of the best things you can do (if you've lost your job) is to understand the various government benefits in your country as well as any kind of financial relief that you qualify for.

Once you identify them, go ahead and apply immediately. During a recession, income is very important and that's why the phrase "cash is king" is often used during a recession. If you fail to secure income from a job, then you must do all it takes to take advantage of every dime you're entitled to from the government.

Let go of all unnecessary spending

I guess this may sound very obvious, but I need to talk about it. One of the most important steps you should take during a recession is to cut all non-essential spending. Although the COVID-19 recession is a bit different since it has caused most countries around the world to lockdown and compel people to stay home. This has significantly led to a reduction in the level of non-essential spending. When you're unable to leave your home, then you won't spend your money on things like transportation, travel, shopping or even eating out. Well, it's not completely impossible to avoid engaging in non-essential spending since Amazon as well as other e-commerce companies have made it easy to buy just about anything online and get it at your doorstep. I encourage you to avoid all non-essential spending for now.

Leverage emerging opportunities

The truth is that there will always be an opportunity in every crisis and this recession is no different. Among the things we are going to expect during a recession is the drop in the price of stocks as well as real estate. We've seen this happen already in different countries but as soon as the COVID-19 crisis is over, the stock market and the economy will certainly recover (which is already happening) and individuals who invest "wisely" and "boldly" will undoubtedly enjoy exceptional returns.

The idea of investing can be scary sometimes, especially when you don't have sufficient information about the stock market, real estate or other sectors. In fact, anyone who isn't scared of investing in times of uncertainty would be seen as reckless. But in times like this, what often comes to my mind are the words of Warren Buffett:

"Be fearful when others are greedy. Be greedy when others are fearful."

I would strongly recommend that if you have a strong emergency fund that can cover your family's expenses for 3-6 months if you lose your income, then one of the best decisions you can make during a recession is to decide on the level of risk that's comfortable for you and invest wisely. If you've not lost your job and you and your partner have over six months worth of emergency funds set aside, then you're undoubtedly in a strong position to invest.

A recession could end up being an opportunity to do things that will move you and your family into a stronger financial position. One of the ways a recession can affect homes is in the possible drop in real estate value. The retirement plan of a good number of homes depends on the value of their homes. Unfortunately, real estate values usually drop drastically with an increase in foreclosures. This compels many families to leave their homes, so we can't really see real estate as a safe investment during a recession. But with time, real estate value may turn around, so if possible, try to maintain ownership of your home. By refinancing mortgages, you can also avoid foreclosure. Tough economic times may actually be ahead, and if you're not fully prepared for it, then you may be worried. This is the time to do all you can to insulate yourself and your family by increasing your earnings. Consider putting in a little overtime and a side hustle which could be online. Freelancing is one of the easiest ways to earn without leaving your home, so if you have services that you can render online, then become a freelancer.

Stock up on cash

There are two aspects of every recession but before I continue, I just want to mention that when you move to cash, you will save yourself the inevitable mental stress that's associated with a falling market. The two aspects of every recession include surviving during an economic downturn and taking advantage of the opportunities that will emerge during and after the recession. But what should be top on your list of to-dos when we're likely to experience a recession is to prepare for emergencies.

Although emergencies tend to happen in expanding economies, we experience more frequent emergencies during recessions. This implies that one of the smartest ways to prepare in advance for a recession is to have a well-stocked emergency fund and you can learn more about how to boost your emergency fund in the next chapter. This is a smart way to prevent a small financial challenge from turning into big ones. The second reason why you need to stock up on cash is to take advantage of opportunities and invest. People will always panic when the financial markets become shaky and many just want to sell everything and move their assets into cash. Unfortunately, this isn't the best strategy during an economic downturn. If you're still employed, then continue to contribute to your 401(K) plans for the long-term. In some countries, opportunities to buy small businesses that are cash strapped have begun to arise and if you have cash and you're currently managing an existing business, then you can buy such businesses. Another reason why cash is king during a recession is that you can easily buy into the market which is often more important in recessions than ever. Have you recently taken a look at the stocks? They all began to drop when the COVID-19 pandemic led to the shutting down of companies and businesses around the world. But the price of these stocks will never remain down forever. According to Anthony Montenegro who is the founder of The Blackmont Group:

"The investment strategy that works best in a recession is to have little to no consumer debt, own cash, and have the guts to buy at the bottom of the dip."

When making decisions, facts will help to boost your confidence level. Did you know that the average stock market loss during bear markets dating back to 1926 has been 30 percent over an average of 1.3 years?

Well, that's just one aspect of the situation, but here is the second aspect; the bull (or upward price movement of stocks) markets after such bear markets have also resulted in an average cumulative return of 339 percent over 6.6 years. This is the surge that you shouldn't miss just because you're scared of the short-term decline in the market. I'll add here that the 2008 recession was perhaps the best year to purchase stocks in several decades.

Reallocate, Restructure and Renegotiate

Do you currently have underperforming assets? One of the things you can do is to cash them out and pay off higher interest rate loans. This is because you may end up paying more interest simply because you lack the right cash flow reporting (which has made it difficult to get the best deals from banks), credit score, the right connections or even collateral. By using equity to offset higher interest rate loans, you can restructure your loans. Another aspect you can consider is to renegotiate your interest rates and don't forget that it's not as difficult as you may think to negotiate a lower rate with credit card companies.

Diversifying your investment is also an excellent idea because that's one way to ensure that all your money is not in one place. Consider building a portfolio of investment pairs that are not too correlated. So, when one investment pair goes up, the other is down – just like stocks and bonds. If you're considering asset classes and stocks, then go for the ones that are not also related to your primary source of income or occupation. The beauty of implementing excellent financial strategies is that they will not only serve you during a recession but will serve you very well regardless of what is happening in the market.

Pay down high-interest debt and watch out for your credit score

You need to take the pressure off your cash flow (especially when you experience financial challenges) by paying down your high-interest debt. When you don't have a massive credit card bill each month, you will have less to worry about until things normalize. But your balances can spike rapidly when you only make the minimum payments on your credit cards and fail to pay down your debt.

Have you considered what will happen if you lose your job, your debt is increasing and you have kids at home to take care of? Well, by taking care of your high-interest debt, you will prevent this from happening. Being concerned about your credit score when you're bothered about a possible economic downturn may appear silly. But have you also thought of the possibility of you being in the position to buy your first home amid the recession? The best time to purchase is when the prices of products and homes are down, however, getting a loan during a recession is a complicated process. During recessions, lenders don't lend to everyone they see – they lend only to the strongest borrowers. What this means is that you might be out of luck if you don't have stellar credit. You just have to always check your credit report regularly to ensure that there is no false report. Generally, economic downturns also come with their opportunity and your goal is not only to survive during such difficult times but to prepare for the opportunities that will emerge after the recession.

Chapter IX

Building up your emergency funds

The first time I decided to set up an emergency fund even before I got married, I was so excited about the idea that I couldn't wait to start. But when I calculated how much I would have as my emergency fund, I simply started talking myself out of the whole thing. How could I manage to save such an amount of money? I knew it would require me to make some life-changing decisions and I wasn't really prepared for it. So, I just spent the money changing my smartphone and on other things that weren't so important to me, after all, I was a bachelor without much responsibility, so I could afford to mess around with my money.

One cold day in winter, I was driving to work in the morning when my car suddenly broke down in the middle of nowhere. I was stranded and needed to get to work and also fix the car, but the fault was a major one that required a huge amount of money. At that point, I realized that if I had started saving my emergency funds, I would have easily resolved this issue. I managed to get to work late and even though I managed to fix my car after waiting for several weeks to raise the money, I dusted my financial goals and agreed to finally do it. I've never looked back since then and my confidence level has increased significantly.

There is no doubt that the backbone of every meaningful personal finance plan is emergency fund. Managing your budget is often a stressful activity especially when you're faced with an unexpected event and that's why every one of us needs to prepare adequately for it. When you have an emergency fund, it's always easy to handle emergencies without accepting family loans, credit card debt or borrowing from other options which can increase your stress level. Your emergency funds can't solve all your money problems, however, it's a great start when it comes to the effective management of your finances. So, what exactly does an emergency fund mean? When defining emergency funds, it's crucial to first understand what it's not:

- An emergency fund doesn't have to be a large and unrealistic amount of money – you can actually start small.
- You don't make use of emergency funds for purchasing things like a new car, a house, for college education and several others.
- There is no specific amount for everyone, instead, emergency funds will always vary based on our lifestyles.

"So, an emergency fund refers to the money that we set aside for unexpected events or problems that will require money."

When you have emergency funds, you also have peace of mind even when you experience something awful like the loss of profit in business or the loss of a job. When you have an emergency fund, you wouldn't be bothered about how to resolve the issues or how you and your family will survive financially.

Now you know why you need an emergency fund. In my opinion, one of the best ways to avoid heart attacks is to have an emergency fund. The truth is that there will always be challenges in life and if you lose your job while having children at home to feed and care for, you easily get worried which might affect your health negatively.

How much should you have as your emergency fund?

The emergency fund of every one of us will certainly vary depending on various conditions. However, most financial experts are of the view that we all need to have a fully-stocked emergency fund that can cover between three to six months of monthly expenses. Others believe that we should set aside funds that will last between three to eight months' worth of household expenses. Well, regardless of the one you choose to go with, they all agree that it's crucial to have some funds for the unexpected. As I mentioned earlier, the amount of money each of us needs to set aside will vary but the first thing you need to do right now to help you determine what you should set aside as your emergency fund is to figure out how much you actually spend monthly.

For those in the United States, consumer expenditure figures that were released by the Bureau of Labor Statistics reveal that in 2017, the average annual expenditure per consumer unit was $60,000. This is also the most recent data as there is none for 2018 and 2019 yet. We shall be working with this rate which I believe will not be the same for other countries. However, this will help you have an idea of how to calculate what you should have as your emergency fund. Now, when we break down the figure by months in a table, you will see how much you're expected to save each month.

Number of Months	Cumulative Monthly Expenses
1	$5,005
2	$10,010
3	$15,015
4	$20,020
5	$25,025
6	$30,030

It's possible to have household expenses that are either lower than the average or higher and a look at these figures shows that having just three months' worth of expenses is big. You don't have to be discouraged by the big number you're seeing here. If you can get the average for your country, then that would be a great idea.

Alternatively, we earlier discussed creating a family budget and one of the things you need to do when creating a budget is to estimate your monthly expenses. So, go ahead and estimate how much you spend on food, groceries, bills and other family expenses each month. Once you identify a figure, then that can also serve as your emergency funds. Simply add it up for six months to give you a rough figure you can work with. Then start small because it's always easier to achieve a smaller goal and in this case, your smaller goal should be to set aside funds for one month. Once you achieve this, then you can proceed to work on the next month and as you do this, you will have this awesome feeling of accomplishment.

When calculating how much you need to set aside as emergency funds, it's crucial to understand how difficult it would be for you to replace your current monthly income. You may have to increase your emergency funds if you work in an industry where it's always very difficult to get a new job. You still need to set aside an emergency fund even if you're a well-qualified employee and you also work in an industry that's easy to get a job.

How to use your emergency founds

Let's be clear on what an emergency fund should be used for; it must be used for expenses that are related to the preservation of your health and assets of your financial future. Examples of genuine financial emergencies that may require the use of an emergency fund include:

- An accident or an unexpected car breakdown
- Job loss
- A member of your family is injured and this demands your time to provide care and support

- The sudden issue with a major aspect of an owned property like an electrical fault, roof problems or air conditioner issues
- Unplanned medical expenses required to maintain your health
- The sudden death of a family member and you need to travel for the funeral immediately.

These are some examples of situations where you can use your emergency fund. So, what are some of the things that you shouldn't regard as emergencies? Consider some examples of expenses that do not justify the use of your emergency fund:

- A last-minute request by a friend or family member for you to travel to a specific destination for a wedding
- Going for elective healthcare such as a plastic surgery
- Having worn-out tires which is a normal aspect of car usage (you need to include this in your budget instead of using your emergency funds)
- Accepting a great deal on a cruise vacation
- Having to change your worn-out carpets in your home
- Buying a new television for Super Bowl because you couldn't save enough for it

Why do you need much funds?

You would agree with me that we live in uncertain times and economies, especially with the COVID-19 pandemic. Presently, corporate loyalty is fast fading away and some companies are already laying off the employees. This makes it very important to have a backup fund to help you overcome the challenges you may face. Well, even when there is no global crisis, people still experience emergencies such as disability, sudden illness, a new roof, major car repairs and other expenses and trust me, there is really never a good time for most of these things to happen. The amount of money you need to save each month may appear to be big, but six months' worth of expenses is so tiny compared to what you need to save for retirement. Three-or-six-months' worth of expenses isn't much compared to what you need to survive for 20 years or more.

Steps to building emergency funds

When setting up your emergency fund, one of the most common mistakes some people do is to start with a big amount. Unfortunately, it's often hard to achieve the goal of setting aside your emergency funds when you start with an unrealistic amount. The truth is that having your living expenses for six months or more is a big goal and it will take you years to accomplish – this depends on your income. So, you're likely going to be disheartened along the way. But there is a smart way to avoid this common pitfall and that's to start with a reasonable goal. For instance, you can make your first target to be $200 or $400 depending on your paycheck. You can easily achieve this goal in a few months or less if you practice some of the smart tips for cutting down your expenses which I will be sharing with you later. Although this amount is quite small, it can still make a lot of difference when you're faced with an emergency. So, if you're going to set $400 as your first target, then break it down to small amounts that you can save each week. This means that at $25 each week, you will hit your target in 16 weeks or about four months. If you want to achieve this goal in ten weeks, then you'll need to put away $40 every week. I don't always put away huge sums of money that can easily discourage me. I prefer saving small amounts that I can conveniently let go while maintaining other things in my budget. I would strongly advise that you shouldn't set your goal too high when you're just starting – both the amount you want to save every week as well as the whole amount you set as your goal. Cutting down on your expenses with the smart tips I shared will increase the amount of money you have for other meaningful goals.

The next step is to automate the entire process. The process of managing your finances is connected and every aspect is very important. Automating the process prevents you from being tempted to spend it on irrelevant things that appear important. In case you're still not sure how to automate your finances, please go through chapter six to understand how you can do it.

Establish tangible milestones!

As you continue to adhere to your resolve to put away a specific amount each week, you need to set tangible milestones. So, if you set your first target of saving $400 in two months, you'll feel good when you hit this milestone. If you keep the money in an interest yielding account, then the money would have started earning you a little interest. Here is one of the good things about having an emergency fund; you begin to have a greater sense of control of the situation. You're no longer scared that if something happens unexpectedly, you may not have the funds to resolve it. Once your confidence level begins to go up, then it's time to set another milestone and this time, consider making it $1000. You need to adopt the same strategy you used for the first target which is to split the amount and have a particular amount you save each week. As soon as you achieve this goal, you can take it a step further (depending on your income) and aim for saving one month's worth of living expenses. Keep increasing this as long as you can handle it until you hit your six months' worth of living expenses.

What happens after you have an emergency fund? You may be tempted to relax and start spending on things you don't really need, especially when you still have the amount you put away each week. You need to include this to your financial goal so you already know what to do when the time comes. You have to continue to live a financially stable life based on your plan. This is the time to search for other ways to save and focus on doing what many millionaires do – make money work for you. If you must invest your money wisely, then you need to at least have something to invest which could be your life savings.

Another reason why you need to continue with your savings is that things could have changed for you. I had a target while I was a bachelor and before I hit my target, I got married. Well, things changed completely because we're now two and would be having kids. The right amount of money for our emergency funds increased and I had to hold a meeting with my partner and discuss our finances. Instead of maintaining the same amount I was putting away each week, we agreed to increase it. The emergency funds you have may no longer cover your expenses because things have changed. So, as you hit your target, you don't have to stop, instead, you may have to increase it if you have a new child at home or when you get married. Also, you might have withdrawn some money from the account to resolve any challenge you had. You need to replace what you've used and don't forget to add all this to your financial plan.

Where do you keep your emergency fund?

This is a very important point to bear in mind – the ideal place to keep your funds. Don't forget that your goal here is to access your cash quickly and easily. This implies that wherever you choose to keep your funds, you can access it when an emergency happens. Among the best places to keep your emergency funds include:

- **A high-yield savings account:** Most high-yield accounts are now found at online banks, but you will have to use another bank account when transferring your funds in and out of your high-yield savings account. This often leads to a delay in accessing your funds, especially when unexpected events happen. However, they are still very accessible and gives you the chance to receive a higher interest rate compared to the traditional savings account. Some high-yield accounts earn between 1-2 percent - though this depends on several factors such as the size of your account.

- Another option is to keep them in a **money market account** which is also similar to a high-yield savings account. While the two earn higher interest rates than traditional banks, they have some differences. Since money market accounts allow you to write checks, they are often a bit more convenient. Perhaps the most remarkable difference between the two is that the money market requires a higher minimum deposit than a high-yield savings account.

- **Certificate of deposit:** You can also keep your emergency funds in a certificate of deposit, but you're expected to keep your money in the account for a particular time to enable you receive a guaranteed rate of return.

You should always see your emergency fund as some kind of insurance policy. As soon as you set it up, you need to guard it carefully so you don't become tempted to spend it wrongly. You don't have to use it for accidental expenses and even when your salary rises, you should also increase the amount you contribute to your emergency fund. Only make use of the fund when you have a real emergency and remember, the moment you spend a part of the money, it usually takes a longer time than you anticipated to replace it. You will always have a better shot at dealing with a crisis when you have an emergency fund.

Chapter X

Building & growing your life savings

One of the greatest benefits I derive from making and managing my money is the sense of security and pride. I don't have any fears of waking up one way and finding it difficult to feed my family just because I was laid off. The confidence I get knowing that I can take care of my needs for the next six months or more until I'm able to figure out what to do next gives me peace of mind.

The habit of setting aside some money as your savings comes naturally to some people who have the "savers" money personality. But for "big spenders," it is a habit that needs to be learned. If you don't have a savings account now, then I encourage you to read this chapter carefully and take action immediately. One big question that often comes to mind when it comes to money management is, how do I make a decision about when to spend and when to save money? I can guarantee you that having the answer to this big question is knowing the secret of having excellent life savings management. This is a skill that one needs to learn as early as possible because it will help you for the rest of your life. Let me also add here that it's never too late or too early to start saving. People sometimes get confused about the difference between life savings and emergency funds. Emergency funds refer to money that is set aside for unplanned expenses such as job loss, unexpected life circumstances, unexpected bills, etc. On the other hand, a savings account has to do with setting aside a specific amount of money for different goals – for investments, education, a home, etc. So, whenever we save, it's usually to help us meet a particular goal that we planned for. Your life savings are not for emergencies or the rainy days; instead, they are the funds you set aside as financial preparation for specific life-changing events. The truth is that your attitude toward the money you earn and set aside as savings, as well as how important your life savings is compared to other things in your life, determines how well you can take control of your life and finance.

So, why build life savings

When I consider my finances, I can comfortably say that I belong to the lower-middle class in terms of my income but I take issues that have to do with life savings seriously. It shouldn't be for the rich alone; instead, everyone can build life savings regardless of personal economics and income status. Here are some goals for starting and growing life savings:

- Career shift
- Education (this could be higher education)
- Relocating

- Independent living (when moving out of home to live alone)
- Homeownership
- Marriage and family
- Major insurance plan
- Retirement
- Property
- Personal financial plans such as long-term travel
- Taking care of your loved ones or elderly parents

As you can see, most of the goals that motivate you to build life savings are directly linked to life-changing events. Also, the process of getting such things or making them happen can involve financial and emotional strain which can be stressful.

Setting up your savings account

You need to consider some important factors before opening a savings account – whether it's your first savings account or not. The perfect time to open a savings account is now. So, if you don't already have one, then you need to shop around for banks right away. When choosing the bank to open a savings account, it's crucial to choose banks that have account insurance. Also, you should choose a bank that provides you a convenient way to check your balance and make it easy to maintain your account.

High-yield Savings account, Traditional Savings account and Personal Safekeeping

Your money will still yield interests as long as it's in your traditional savings account. But high-yield accounts can actually offer you higher interest rates than traditional accounts, however, they also have various requirements. For instance, high-yield accounts may have specific restrictions on deposit sizes or minimum balances. Here are some of the benefits of keeping your life savings in a bank:

- You can earn some interest which will help to grow your money.
- Keeping your life savings in the bank is the safest as well as the easiest choice.
- With the availability of online banking, it's very convenient because you can monitor your progress via your monthly statements and this helps you maintain proper and accurate records.

The major challenge with keeping your life savings in the bank is that you may be tempted to touch the money since there are no restrictions.

Another alternative is to put your money in a time deposit or pension plan. This option ensures that your money will grow faster than the traditional bank account because of the high-interest rates. But you can't touch this money until a specific time. For people who are big spenders, this comes as an excellent option since it helps to curb their spending issues. But this option comes with its merits and demerits. Some people also prefer keeping their money by themselves – stashed away somewhere secret and in their home. The best choice for those who decide to keep their money is a deposit box. The benefit of keeping your money is that you can easily access your funds when you need them.

However, your money will not have an interest and if you're an elderly person, then you may end up forgetting where you kept the money. Even if your money is in a locked and safe place, anything can happen to it. Your decision on which of the type of account you should use depends on factors such as your income, goal for having the life savings, etc. Another thing you need to consider is the issue of fees. Avoid opening an account with banks that charge extra fees – but don't also confuse these fees with excessive withdrawal fees. There is no point in paying a bank to allow you save money in an account. To avoid having issues with your savings account, make sure you go through all fees that are associated with the opening of an account. Don't forget that you might be charged some fees for withdrawing more than the maximum number of times in a month. Find out what your account limit is as well as the fees charged in case you exceed it. Watch out for banks that offer "giveaways," because they are among the biggest traps that banks set for customers. You may get an offer to enjoy a free pizza when you open an account or a gift card. I would recommend that you choose the best account for you and not necessarily the ones offering you something just to sign up.

Steps to setting up your savings account

Now that you understand some basic things about opening a savings account, how do you start saving? Just before I continue, I want to take you back to the beginning of this book. I started with the main reason why most people mismanage their finances as well as common money mindsets. The reason why I started with the money mindset is that the core factor that will determine how well you manage all other aspects of financial management is your mindset. You can never maintain a life savings without first learning how to control your expenses. Also, I talked about the importance of having a family budget which helps you plan how you spend your money effectively. While budgeting, you also need to set aside some funds not only for your emergency funds but for your life savings.

Now you see how connected all the chapters are? The first step toward setting up your savings is to have a good budget because that's the easiest way to make a budget and stick to it. So, while making your budget, ensure you set aside a specific amount you plan to move into your life savings account. It's crucial to separate your savings account from your checking account. In fact, consider using two different banks for your savings and checking account to discourage you from spending the money you wanted to save.

One of the things I talked about earlier in this book is how to automate your finances. The best way to ensure your savings account grows steadily is to automate deposits to your account. So, before you even get the money from your paycheck, your savings would have been deducted. What if your current income is barely enough to cover your expenses? Well, there are smart ways to cut your expenses, so go back to the section on how to spend less than your paycheck. Another option you have is to increase your income, especially if you find it difficult to cut down on the money you spend on the things you enjoy.

People have different motives for having their savings. I often have savings for different goals, so when planning a vacation, I have a separate savings account for that purpose. This also applies to other goals. If you desire to have your home when you are at the age of 37 and expect to have saved at least $150,000 which represents the average cost of owning a home, then it means that you have tied your savings to a major life goal and you also have deadlines too. But some people save and allow their accounts to grow continuously without having a particular major life goal earmarked for the money. This is not entirely a bad idea because time for using the funds will eventually come. But having a goal in mind before setting up a savings account will help to increase your commitment to building and maintaining the account. Regardless of your strategy – whether a target savings or saving without a particular goal – one thing is sure and that's you have a savings which you can always use when the right opportunity comes. The option you choose depends on your view about life goals as well as your circumstances.

Maintaining your life saving account

Perhaps what's more important when it comes to your life savings account is not how much money you have in it but your mindset about your life savings. In my opinion, this is what I think will be the difference between just setting aside some amount of money in your savings account and looking forward to the future where you achieve your financial goals. If you don't have specific plans for setting aside a life savings fund, you can easily get sidetracked by using the funds for different purposes that are not so important or by not being so committed to adding up the amount you save. Having a clear goal for saving your money will serve as a compelling reason to build your life savings and maintain it even as you look forward to using it for its purpose in the future.

Funding your life savings

Identifying the importance of setting some funds aside for major purposes is good, but you also need to come up with a plan to help you increase the funds. So, how do you get the funds for your savings account? One way to ensure that the money in your account grows consistently is by having different sources of income *"contribute"* to your life savings fund. However, this is for those who have multiple sources of income. The income shouldn't just be from paychecks, incentives from special projects or money you realized from cutting down on your expenses. It's often easier to make earnings and timeline projections. Your goal accomplishment will be achievable when you clearly understand the major sources of funds for your life savings. You need to establish a strict and regular schedule or routine for moving funds into your account, especially if you're also maintaining an emergency basket and standard savings account. If you have budgeted expenses and fixed savings, then it's sensible enough to allot your money from your paycheck to your standard savings as I earlier mentioned in automating your finances.

The truth is that a life savings fund (which is often preparing for major life events or big-ticket items) requires a lot of time and planning. This also applies to the life savings which is meant to accomplish long term projects – gradual but big. One way to allocate funds to your emergency funds, standard savings and life savings is by creating a schedule for injecting funds into your life savings. You can schedule it to coincide with expected income such as cash tax reimbursements, bonuses at work, earnings from an investment you made, profit sharing and other similar "collectibles." You can even choose to add a portion of your monthly paycheck if that's convenient for you. But the reason why you need to have a schedule is that it will help you to stick to your plan to grow your funds and avoid possible conflicts that may arise when setting aside funds for your emergency funds as well as your standard savings. Having a schedule helps to eliminate possible pressures since you're certain that you will receive money for a specific purpose and already know how to use it. Make sure you come up with a schedule and stick to it.

Growing your funds

Since life savings are meant for major life goals and are mainly long-term, you can maximize the value of your funds by exploring its potential growth. However, you just have to be careful when choosing how to "invest" your life savings. An excellent option is to go for investment-linked savings, but also use the ones with low risk or those that offer guaranteed returns on investments such as a certificate of deposit. Most of the no-risk products available will allow you to withdraw your funds before its maturity date, but with a penalty. I just love saving my money with low or no risk products because I already have an emergency fund which is set aside for unexpected expenses. So, it's rare to touch my life savings since I already have a separate account for emergencies so I just enjoy guaranteed returns on investments.

Another option is to *"diversify"* your life savings based on potential growth and security. So, you can invest a portion of your funds in the low-risk money market while keeping the other portion for guaranteed interest investments. In fact, you can have a third chunk of your funds in the bank or anywhere you want that's safe from the volatile market forces.

Chapter XI

Leveraging technology to manage your finances

There are several ways that technology can assist you to manage your money, save on most of the purchases you make every day and create a better budget. While talking about budgeting, I mentioned that you can leverage some tools to make the process easy and I'll be sharing some excellent budgeting tools you need later. It's important to know that each of these tools make up a crucial component of a holistic financial plan. One of the good things about these tools is that they are software programs that will not clutter your home like the gadgets we often buy. It appears that we now have a software program for almost every purpose, especially when it comes to managing your money. Now, it's possible to track your expenses, receive money, send payments, bank, budget, send invoices and even find out our credit score online – we can do all these things from the comfort of our home. However, it's usually challenging for the less tech savvy individuals who are mainly seniors to learn how to make use of new technology. In fact, a survey by Chapman University shows that in the United States, about 15 percent of them are scared of technology they don't understand. Well, if you're not comfortable with new technology, especially software programs on smartphones, then I would strongly suggest that you do what you're comfortable with.

Using the traditional way of managing our finances which involves a lot of paperwork is still a good one provided you take action on the things I have shared. So, if you're comfortable with new technology, then let's explore some tools that will help you manage your finances better.

Searching for the best price for goods and services

Apart from trying some generic products, another excellent way to increase the value you get for your money is to ensure that you're actually paying the best price for a product or service. Sometimes, when buying something from the grocery store in person, we end up paying more than what we would have paid if we bought them online. With apps such as Barcode scanner on your smartphone, it's now possible to know whether the product you want to buy is available and cheaper elsewhere. All you need to do is to take a photo of the bar-code. Once you discover that you can get it cheaper online, then you will save more money that you would have spent buying it in person.

You can actually take it a step further by checking websites such as Deals Plus and Coupon Follow where you can get discount sales that offer a percentage off the price of the items you want to buy or free delivery. However, these services may not be available to all countries, but you can check to know if it's available in your location. did you also know that some apps such as Fuelio can take things a step further by helping you to calculate the cost of driving from one point to the other where you can buy things? These apps can make you a savvy shopper and increase your savings.

Take advantage of promotions

One of the things you can enjoy when you shop around and go through various websites for promotions is that you will cut down on your expenses significantly. While buying from your booking sites, favorite stores and others, try to sign up for their newsletter. This is usually what they use in informing their customers of promotions that you can enjoy.

Energy savings opportunity

It's also possible to save some of the money you spend on energy bills by using your smartphone. All you have to do is to find out whether your current tariff is the best one for you. Websites such as Choose Energy and several others can help you compare all energy providers in your location (remember, this may not be in all countries) and come up with the cheapest deals for you. In fact, the site will take the stress of switching energy providers away from you by switching on your behalf with just a few clicks. This can end up saving you hundreds of dollars annually. Apps like Fuelio will show you the current fuel prices of the gas stations close to you to help you decide on the cheapest and most convenient one.

Monitor your bank account

It's easy to spend more than you have planned when you're not working with a plan. It's easier for you to keep an eye on your expenses by using smartphone apps that can show you your bank account balance. If you want to monitor the progress of your life savings and emergency funds, then mobile banking apps can help you do that easily. With your bank's mobile app, you can send payments, view your transaction history and request refunds. There are other apps that provide calculators designed to assist you in determining your net worth, making any investment decisions, estimating your insurance needs, calculating the time value of your funds and even offering guidance on various financial issues.

Track your budget on the go

I've shared several tips on how you can create a family budget in chapter six. But you should bear in mind that personal finance is a combination of several components which include your family budget. Creating a budget for yourself is important but being consistent with the financial goals that you've made is equally important. Monitoring your budget will help to ensure that you haven't exceeded the boundary you set for yourself, especially boundaries related to your purchases. Online budgeting apps will always guide you and help you adhere to your budget.

Possible downsides of technology

Just like every other thing, technology still has its downside and it's important that you know them to save you from being the next victim.

- **Issue of security breach:** There has been a recent increase in the cases of online security breaches in different cities around the world. In fact, banks as well as shopping establishments have been hacked which ends up putting their customers at risk. However, there are several ways to protect yourself against identity theft and one of them is to always be up to date with news and remain conscious of your online activity. Before you download an app, it's important to confirm its authenticity because several apps have been used to obtain people's personal information.

- **Security issues:** Technology has provided the comfort we need when accessing its features, but it also seems to be addictive. For instance, information from WashingtonTimes.com reveals that on average, each person spends about five hours daily with their smartphones. Unfortunately, if you're not careful, you may spend most of your time on various social media sites such as Facebook, Instagram and several others posting or checking other people's posts and this could significantly reduce your level of productivity. Already, you're trying to manage the little money you earn so you shouldn't allow technology to deprive you of income opportunities. Social life is very good, especially during the COVID-19 era with calls for social distancing. But always make sure that it doesn't take up a good amount of time from your work.

- **Avoid being too dependent on technology:** Another downside of technology has to do with developing an unhealthy dependence on technology. Some people actually get to the point where they can no longer function without their smartphones. While enjoying the convenience and other benefits of your technology, always remember that technology is simply a tool that can help make life a bit easier for you. Your gadgets can help you accomplish your tasks and smartphones ensure that you communicate with others. However, you're not some kind of robot that depends on technology to function; you're still a human being.

Social engineering

Initially, the strategy that scammers use was to call people and identify themselves as officers of an organization or a bank, then provide their ID and rank to appear as credible as possible. The next step would be to ask you to provide your bank account details as well as your personal identification number. Then they would ask you some security questions and if you provide the answers to the questions, then you may be giving them the information they need. But scammers noticed that this was no longer working, so rather than call, they would send an SMS from the "bank" or "organization" informing people of a privacy breach that has compromised their information. Then they would ask them to visit the bank's website and verify their identity. Of course, they would provide a link that will lead to a page that doesn't look suspicious at first since it's quite similar to the real page. Unfortunately, it's not the real page but was properly designed to appear as the real website of the bank. This is how they get peoples' personal information. There is now a recent strategy which you need to be aware of, especially when trying to manage your finances with mobile apps. Scammers now send people a link, not to a phishing page but a page that would ask them to download an app that also looks real. Users are requested to download and install the app, then provide their details by filling the app and as soon as the information is provided, they would use it to transfer all the funds in the account. So, you should be careful when downloading apps or clicking on suspicious links. Don't provide sensitive information like your passwords, CVV numbers or PINs to people on the phone who claim to be bank employees. Always bear in mind that banks would never request such information. You need to have a good security app installed on your smartphone to warn you of fake apps and phishing sites. Before you click on links that are attached to messages or emails, always type the link manually. Alternatively, search for the company's official website via Google and copy the correct link.

Most scams are not always trying to compromise your security settings or hack your phone (though this happens sometimes), but scammers attempt to get people's information. To avoid becoming a victim of a mobile scam, you need to change some of your daily habits and be conscious of who you share your personal information with.

- Always make use of authorized apps like your bank's official app or site instead of clicking a link that was sent to you.

- Avoid storing your personal information like your PINs or sharing them through an email or message.

- Remember to always lock the screen of your smartphone with a passcode to prevent others from having easy access to your information.

- Sometimes, I get tired of updating mobile apps on my smartphone, but since I learned that the updates help protect the phone from scammers, I have never failed to update my apps as well as the operating system of my mobile device. The updates of your phone's operating system sometimes come with improved security settings for your smartphone and even resolve several vulnerabilities so always keep it updated.

- With the availability of Wi-Fi hotspots, we're always connected and this makes others easily gain access to our information. You must avoid entering PINs or passwords when you're in public places.

- In the event that you want to let go of your mobile device, ensure that you reset it back to the factory settings. This will erase all your data on the phone. Also, don't forget to remove your MicroSD card if you have one and make sure that you're not leaving any personal information for the next user to see.

It's a lot easier to control and manage your personal finance with the help of technology. But you still have to make the financial decisions that will help you attain your goals in life. Even though technology helps you to automate your finances and makes suggestions for you, the real decision-making rests solely on you.

Managing your finances in the past has always been limited to speaking with a professional who helped you to invest in bonds, stocks, etc. and having a close relationship with your local bank. Undoubtedly, these traditional money management methods are still relevant and valuable, however, technology has provided us with more options that would help us to manage our finances more efficiently. I'm not in any way suggesting that you abandon the traditional money management habits because they have shown overtime to be effective. What I do is combine the two techniques and habits to enable me get the best out of my money.

Chapter XII

Investing even when you're not earning enough

It's always crucial to make hay while the sun still shines, so while saving, you also need to invest part of your funds at the right time. Having the right savings will ensure that your future remains bright. The truth is that the difficult challenges we're facing with the economy will not last forever, but you're also not getting younger. Having limited financial resources is not a crime; in fact, being born to a poor family is no crime. But in my opinion, being stagnant and staying that way is wrong. There is this wrong belief that for us to start saving or investing, we need to have a huge sum of money or an excellent source of income. This is completely untrue because the process of building a solid portfolio doesn't require a fat bank account. You can actually start with a thousand dollars or less. You can maximize your resources regardless of how small or big it may be. So, how do you go about investing while you're not earning enough? The starting point to the process of investment is SAVINGS!

Earlier, I talked about how you can build your life savings in the chapter X. But I'll just mention that the source of any stable wealth is savings because it will help pave the way for greater wealth. When it comes to investing, it's always better to save from the little amount you're earning and have enough to invest than to take a loan and invest. If you're a committed saver, you can easily create a line of investments because as they always say, what makes an ocean are the little drops of water.

I've already shared tips on how to automate your finances and that's an excellent way to boost your savings especially if you lack the willpower. You shouldn't see investing as a get-rich-quick program because you will only make costly mistakes, especially with your limited resources. Instead, you need to see it as a way to accumulate wealth gradually and consistently. Compound interest makes it possible for small sums of money to turn into fortunes with time as long as you make the right investment decisions. It's often regarded as the "Eight Wonder of the World" because you can grow a few dollars into millions of dollars if given enough time. For instance, if you're 22 years and you start investing $50 each month into your 401K while your employer matches it with a 50 percent contribution. You will end up having over $1 million when you are 65 years with an 8.5 percent return on your 401K investments and annual raises of 3.5 percent. Well, there are other factors to consider when making this estimate, but this will serve as a simple example to illustrate the power of compound interest as long as everything goes well.

The best time to invest

You will discover that if you're waiting for an ideal time to start investing which would be when you start earning a fat paycheck, then you may end up missing out on the time factor. The perfect time to start investing even while you're not earning enough is NOW! As you manage to make effective use of your funds and cut down on your excess daily and monthly expenses, you should not only set some funds aside as your emergency funds and your savings; you also need to have something to invest. There would always be a potential risk for loss when considering the issue of investing, but have you also considered the possibility of a bigger potential for massive gains? If you've not considered investing before, then the idea may be terrifying, especially when you're having financial challenges.

Possible ways to invest money

There are several options available for anyone who desires to invest their money. My experience with stocks has been an exciting one. While it wasn't a convenient thing for me, I have managed to get involved with some investments which I will be sharing with you shortly. One of the things I discovered was that it's always a smart idea to explore different options. I learned that it's a wise thing to consider low-risk and high-risk investments. I focused more on low-risk options considering my limited resources and just set aside a little for investments with more risks. Although I've not lost my investments in the high-risk options, it's often better to be careful especially when I don't have all the money in the world. Please note that I didn't invest in all the options below and I've not added the high-risk investment vehicles that I did. My goal is not to trade stocks (which is often the most glamorized type of investing) but long-term investing. Long-term investing has to do with allowing your money to compound in the stock market for more than 10 and 20 years. One of the best ways people retire rich is through long term value investing, unlike short-term investors who trade in and out of stocks within a short period instead of purchasing and holding for many years. This strategy will always require a bit of luck to be successful. It also comes with more risks as you may lose more than your profit. You should also consider choosing a low-risk option and focus more on it while investing less of your funds in high-risk options.

Investing in the stock market

Perhaps the most beneficial and even the most common investment that people put their money is the stock market. Buying a stock will enable you to own a small portion of the company. So, the company may pay part of the profits they made as dividends when they make a profit and this will be distributed based on the number of shares you own. The price of the stock will increase as its value grows which also means that if you choose to sell the stocks later, you will make a profit.

Savings accounts

Although this remains the least risky way to invest your money, it is undoubtedly one of the worst ways to invest your funds and get interest. Low risk implies low returns and there is usually little or no returns when you put your money in a savings account. But it will serve as a great tool for you to stockpile your cash when building your emergency funds. One of the disadvantages of keeping your funds in a savings account is that the value will depreciate with the rate of inflation which may erode the little interest it generated.

Investment bonds

Whenever you purchase a bond, what you're actually doing is to loan your money to the government or a company. In some countries such as the United States, it's possible for people to buy not just government bonds but foreign bonds too. When you buy a company or government bond, you will be entitled to interest on the "loan" which would be based on the bond's lifecycle. While bonds are regarded as less risky than stocks, they also have lower yields for investors.

Physical commodities

This is one of my most favorite options which is to invest in physical commodities like silver or gold. When you have such commodities, they help to safeguard you against difficult times such as the current economic crisis. For instance, the price of gold has been on the increase for several years now. This means that if you had purchased it while its price was low, then you would eventually make a profit by selling now that its value has appreciated.

Certificate of deposit

This option is often regarded as one of the safest investment vehicles available, especially for those who want to avoid high-risk investments. To open a CD investment, sometimes all that's required is a minimum of $500 or $1000 and you will enjoy consistent interest for the duration of the investment. When compared to the ordinary bank savings account, CDs offer higher interest rates. In most cases, the higher rates apply to those who leave more of their funds until it gets to its maturity date and this could be from three months to ten years. This is a great option for your life savings because, unlike your emergency funds, you may not use your life savings until a specific time when you need it. So, if you're choosing this option, consider the right term length to enable you to gain access to the funds. In case you decide to also use your emergency funds, then consider opening a no-penalty CD to avoid paying the early withdrawal penalties associated with withdrawing your funds before the agreed time.

How to avoid investment mistakes

"You must learn from the mistakes of others. You can't possibly live long enough to make them all yourself."
– Sam Levenson

Remember, our focus is on how to manage money even when you don't have enough. So, if you've followed up each of the chapters we've earlier discussed, you will realize that you will gradually begin to have free money that you can use for other purposes.

We have talked about understanding your money personality, working on your lifestyle (which has led to unnecessary spending of your money), and learning to spend less than you earn. Also, we've talked about budgeting and how to clear your debts. It's equally important that as you explore various ways to invest that you don't end up losing your funds. Although the rate of fraud in society has continued to increase, one of the most common mistakes people make when investing is making the wrong choice or trying to get rich quick. So, you just have to be smart and careful. Here are a few things about investing which you need to bear in mind:

- **Your investment style should match your personal goals:** The truth is that there isn't a single correct answer to the investment strategy that will benefit everyone. Instead, there is one that's suitable for you and you have to identify it. That someone else is making money by using a particular strategy doesn't mean that you must include the same strategy. Our paths in life are different and one of the best ways to manage your funds even when you're not earning enough is to discover the one that works best for you.

- **Have a plan:** Another mistake that many people do is to invest without a plan. All that we have been talking about in this book has to do with creating a plan to make your limited financial resources work for you. So, while planning your spending, you also need to have a plan for your investment. Results from several studies have shown that individuals who are methodical enough to come up with a well laid out investment plan can expect to do better than their peers by multiples. So, as you decide to set aside some money for investing, also come up with a disciplined plan that will help you achieve your goals. Avoid investing based on hot tips, rumors, future predictions or stories. Your plan should have what is known as positive expectancy.

- **Make it fun:** The reason for this is that wealth is a journey that should be enjoyed and not a destination to be reached. As I earlier pointed out, we have touched on several aspects of life as we work toward living a better life and none of them is a destination. It's a process that involves several aspects of life and you need to follow the process carefully. Since it is a process, you should also find ways to enjoy the experience. You can see investing as a kind of treasure hunt – just like playing Monopoly but this time with real money and rules you make by yourself.

Avoid investing your funds in something you don't understand. Before committing your funds to an investment, make sure you understand what it is and how it works. I would encourage that before you make any investment decisions, you have to do your research on the different options available. All investments have some form of risk and even keeping your funds at home comes with its risk too. What you need to do is to understand your risk tolerance level before committing your funds to an investment vehicle. If possible, consider working with a financial advisor to get more support and also help with how to practice smart investment strategies that will enable you to optimize your investments while limiting your risk.

Final thoughts

Have you observed that every chapter in this book is connected to the others? We started by looking at the importance of having the right money mindset. I have been able to establish that the reason why many people struggle financially is because of their poor money management skills. If you are given a huge amount of money to settle all your debts right now, chances are that you will accumulate more debts within a few months. This is because of your money management skills – your financial habits. If you must overcome your money problems, then first deal with your mindset about money which is the foundation. Once you have established the right foundation, then you can move on to the next step.

I explained how you can identify your spending habits and ways to control it. The way you spend money will always determine whether you will build your emergency funds as well as a life savings account. But knowing what to do may not really be enough to ensure that you control your spending and that's where automating your finance comes in. When you automate your financial life, you drastically reduce your tendency to spend on the wrong things and compel yourself to be financially disciplined. It's the easiest way to prevent your emotions from influencing your decisions. Knowing how to automate your finances will enable you pay yourself first just as the government will do whenever your paycheck is ready.

Paying yourself first will also help you increase your savings and boost your confidence. But you also need to cut down on your expenses to ensure that you're not spending on the wrong things. Your goal is to eliminate all unnecessary expenses and focus more on the truly important ones.

When you don't have a plan, then you're actually planning to fail. So, you need to have a good family budget to help you plan your expenses and manage your funds. Having the right mindset, a good budget, learning how to control your money personality and spending less than what you earn will equip you with what you need to get rid of your debts. When you pay off your debts, you already have the right money skills to live without accumulating debts. This time, you begin to build your emergency fund and life savings. I believe you're now seeing the whole picture – every strategy is connected to the other.

After reading this book the first time, I strongly recommend that you go through the notes you have written and start again from chapter one. Adopt the *"read and practice"* strategy to ensure that you get the best results. Managing your finances and living a comfortable life is not rocket science – it requires a deliberate effort on your part to be financially stable. This is not an instant remedy to your debt problems and you will not get rich overnight with these strategies. However, I can guarantee that if you make these strategies a lifestyle, then you will definitely enjoy true financial freedom.

Thanks for reading! If you enjoyed this book or found it useful I'd be very grateful if you'd post a short review on Amazon. Your support really does make a difference and I read all the reviews personally so I can get your feedback and make this book even better.

Thanks again for your support!

References

Africa's Pocket. (January 6, 2020). What is your money personality? Retrieved on May 5, 2020, from https://medium.com/@info_92632/what-is-your-money-personality-bbf00ae8d144

Al. (n.d). 6 Examples of how technology can help Personal Finance. Retrieved on September 29, 2020, from https://www.debtconsolidationusa.com/personal-finance/6-examples-how-technology-can-help-personal-finance.html

Anspach, D. (August 28, 2020). Safe Investments That Can Help Keep Your Money Secure. Retrieved on September 29, 2020, from https://www.thebalance.com/boring-safe-savings-account-2388905

Berger, R. (June 29, 2020). 4 Budget Types and the Best Tools for Each One. Retrieved on September 29, 2020, from https://www.doughroller.net/budgeting/4-budget-types-tools-one/

Bieber, C. (September 18, 2018). 20 Ways to Cut Spending. Retrieved on May 16, 2020, from https://www.fool.com/personal-finance/2018/09/18/20-ways-to-cut-spending.aspx

Briseno, T. (n.d). What's the No. 1 reason people go into debt? Retrieved on May 29, 2020, from https://money.howstuffworks.com/personal-finance/debt-management/reason-people-go-into-debt.htm

Brison, S. (n.d). Money Personalities: What is Your Money Modus Operandi? Retrieved on May 5, 2020, from https://www.listenmoneymatters.com/money-personalities/

Burnette, M. (March 20, 2020). Emergency Fund: What It Is and Why It Matters. Retrieved on May 19, 2020, from Emergency Fund: What It Is and Why It Matters

Caldwell, M. (April 18, 2020). Reasons Why You Should Budget Your Money. Retrieved on May 5, 2020, from https://www.thebalance.com/reasons-to-budget-money-2385699

Calonia, J. (March 23, 2020). Average American Debt. Retrieved on June 6, 2020, from https://www.bankrate.com/finance/debt/average-american-debt/

Chappelow, J. (April 24, 2020). 7 Ways to Recession-Proof Your Life. Retrieved on May 15, 2020, from https://www.investopedia.com/articles/pf/08/recession-proof-your-life.asp

Cothern, L. (May 6, 2020). Emergency Funds: Everything You Need To Know. Retrieved on May 19, 2020, from https://www.moneyunder30.com/emergency-fund

Dafina. (January 16, 2020). How To Change Your Money Mindset So You Can Have More Money. Retrieved on May 13, 2020, from https://dollarsplussense.com/change-your-money-mindset/

Discover. (n.d). 4 Steps to Start an Emergency Fund From Zero. Retrieved on May 21, 2020, from https://www.discover.com/online-banking/banking-topics/4-steps-to-start-an-emergency-fund/

Esaajian, J. D. (n.d). Defining Your Money Mindset. Retrieved on May 21, 2020, from https://www.fortunebuilders.com/money-mindset/

Fisher, S. (August 1, 2019). Fixed Expenses vs. Variable Expenses for Budgeting. Retrieved on June 5, 2020, from https://smartasset.com/financial-advisor/fixed-expenses

Firemum. (July 31, 2020). 12 ways to prepare for a recession. Retrieved on May 15, 2020, from https://www.afamilyonfire.com/12-ways-to-prepare-for-a-recession/

Gage, D. (October 19, 2012). How to make a family budget. Retrieved on May 28, 2020, from https://www.todaysparent.com/family/how-to-make-a-family-budget/

Gilbert, N. (n.d). How to Build and Grow Your Life Savings. Retrieved on June 5, 2020, from https://financesonline.com/how-to-build-and-grow-your-life-savings/

Gilbert, N. (n.d). Simple and Easy Steps To Take Control of Your Life Savings. Retrieved on June 5, 2020, from https://financesonline.com/simple-and-easy-steps-to-take-control-of-your-life-savings

Guina, R. (March 18, 2019). Spending Less Than You Earn is the Key to Building Wealth. Retrieved on May 13, 2020, from https://cashmoneylife.com/spend-less-than-you-earn/

Gunderson, G. (April 4, 2020). How To Make Money During A Recession. Retrieved on May 15, 2020, from https://www.forbes.com/sites/garrettgunderson/2020/04/04/how-to-make-money-during-a-recession/#746bcac83e1b

Hands on Banking (n.d). Budgets and spending plans. Retrieved on June 5, 2020, from https://handsonbanking.org/articles/budgets-spending-plans/

Hamm, T. (March 2, 2020). 40 Ways to Save Money on Monthly Expenses. Retrieved on May 16, 2020, from https://www.thesimpledollar.com/save-money/trimming-the-fat-forty-ways-to-reduce-your-monthly-required-spending/

Hamm, T. (March 13, 2020). A Guide to Building an Emergency Fund. Retrieved on May 21, 2020, from https://www.thesimpledollar.com/investing/blog/a-step-by-step-guide-to-building-a-big-healthy-emergency-fund/

Hefner, J. (nd). Getting Out of Debt: A Step-by-step Guide. Retrieved on June 4, 2020, from https://militarysaves.org/images/stories/pdf/materialstepbystep.pdf

Henshaw, S. (March 22, 2019). The Most Common Mobile Phone Scams & How to Avoid Them. Retrieved on September 29, 2020, from https://www.tigermobiles.com/faq/common-mobile-phone-scams/

Investopedia. (March 29, 2020). How to Build an Emergency Fund. Retrieved on May 19, 2020, from https://www.investopedia.com/personal-finance/how-to-build-emergency-fund/

Jackson, R. (n.d). 6 Ways to Instill a Positive Money Mindset. Retrieved on May 21, 2020, from https://www.mint.com/vip-content/6-ways-to-instill-a-positive-money-mindset

Lake, R. (October 27, 2019). Smart Investing on a Small Budget. Retrieved on September 28, 2020, from https://www.investopedia.com/articles/personal-finance/123115/best-ways-invest-500-5000.asp

Lansat, M. (June 14, 2018). How to start saving money today, even if you think you have nothing to spare. Retrieved on June 5, 2020, from https://www.businessinsider.com/when-to-open-a-savings-account-financial-planner-advice-2018-6

LaPonsie, M. (April 18, 2019). How to Make a Family Budget. Retrieved on May 14, 2020, from https://money.usnews.com/moncy/personal-finance/saving-and-budgeting/articles/how-to-make-a-family-budget

Le Fort, B. (April 1, 2020). How to Survive a Recession and Come out Stronger. Retrieved on May 15, 2020, from https://medium.com/makingofamillionaire/how-to-survive-a-recession-and-come-out-stronger-1e00820e2534

Lifehack. (n.d). 30 Ways To Cut Your Monthly Expenses. Retrieved on May 16, 2020, from https://www.lifehack.org/articles/money/30-ways-cut-your-monthly-expenses.html

Maldonado, C. (October 4, 2019). 7 Things You Need To Do To Prepare For A Potential Recession. Retrieved on May 15, 2020, from https://www.forbes.com/sites/camilomaldonado/2019/10/04/7-things-prepare-for-recession/#3068ffa5518b

Mint. (n.d). How to Create a Family Budget (Easy Step-By-Step Budgeting). Retrieved on May 14, 2020, from https://www.mint.com/budgeting-3/how-to-create-a-budget-step-by-step

Nair, S. (April 15, 2020). New banking scam tricks. Retrieved on September 29, 2020, from https://www.kaspersky.co.in/blog/verification-app-scam/20628/

Pant, P. (June 25, 2019). What Does It Mean to Pay Yourself First? Retrieved on May 13, 2020, from https://www.thebalance.com/what-does-pay-yourself-first-mean-453696

Posner, C. (n.d). What are Fixed, Savings and Variable Costs and Expenses, and How Will They Help Me Learn How to Budget My

Money Properly? Retrieved on June 5, 2020, from
https://www.mymoneycoach.ca/blog/what-are-fixed-savings-variable-costs-expenses-and-learn-to-budget-money.html

Quilty, D. (n.d). 9 Effects of the Recession on Families and How to Cope. Retrieved on May 15, 2020, from
https://www.moneycrashers.com/effects-recession-families/

Rose, J. (February 6, 2020). How To Prepare For The Next Great Recession Of 2020. Retrieved on May 15, 2020, from
https://www.forbes.com/sites/jrose/2020/02/06/how-to-prepare-for-the-next-great-recession-of-2020/

Royal, J. (September 1, 2020). 8 best low-risk investments in September 2020. Retrieved on September 29, 2020, from
https://www.bankrate.com/investing/low-risk-investments/

Sallin, M. (September 14, 2017). How to automate your finances and feel good about money. Retrieved on May 14, 2020, from
https://medium.com/the-mission/how-to-automate-your-finances-and-feel-good-about-money-538d73c79548

Smith, L. (August 4, 2019). What Is Your Money Personality Type? Retrieved on May 7, 2020, from
https://www.investopedia.com/articles/basics/07/money-personality.asp

Torrieri, M. (July 24, 2014). Are You Paying Yourself First? The Money Habit That Can Boost Wealth. Retrieved on May 13, 2020, from https://www.forbes.com/sites/learnvest/2014/07/24/are-you-paying-yourself-first-the-money-habit-that-can-boost-wealth/#44802934732c

Town, P. (n.d) How to Invest Money: A Simple Guide to Grow Your Wealth in 2020. Retrieved on September 28, 2020, from https://www.ruleoneinvesting.com/blog/how-to-invest/how-to-invest-money/

Wagner, T. (n.d). Benefits and Drawbacks Of Automating Your Finances. Retrieved on May 12, 2020, from http://www.leavedebtbehind.com/lifestyle/organization/benefits-and-drawbacks-of-automating-your-finances/

Waits, K. (December 7, 2016). 7 Reasons You Really Need to Pay Yourself First (Seriously). Retrieved on May 13, 2020, from https://www.wisebread.com/7-reasons-you-really-need-to-pay-yourself-first-seriously

Wall Street. (April 9, 2018). Managing your Finances with technology. Retrieved on September 29, 2020, from https://wall-street.com/how-technology-can-make-managing-your-finances-easier/

Weliver, D. (September 13, 2020). 7 Easy Ways to Start Investing with Little Money. Retrieved on September 28, 2020, from moneyunder30.com/start-investing-with-little-money

About the author

Patrick A. Simon is the author of four amazing books and has been exploring the world of writing since 2017. Born in the early '80s, he embraced pedagogy as a major field of study though he still devotes his time to other areas of study, especially economics. Being a dad and having a master's degree in pedagogy, he has acquired extensive experiences throughout his life, which serves as inspiration for his books. This has also helped him to effectively communicate and connect with his readers by writing in a light and straightforward tone that people can easily read and understand.

He loves writing about topics related to paternity, budgeting and personal management. His first book *"Soon to be DAD: Handbook For Expectant Fathers"* explores pregnancy from a male perspective. He wrote the book mainly for expectant dads who appear to be ignored during their significant other's pregnancy to help them understand the kind of experiences they will be having. The book provides an account of his experience with his wife's pregnancy and provides tips and advice to help readers who may be going through a similar situation. As a continuation of the first book, he published his second informative book,

"Couvade Syndrome: What Male Sympathetic Pregnancy is & how you can Fight it." While the first one focused mainly on what soon-to-be dads should expect when their partner gets pregnant, the second one took it a step further. It focused on why soon-to-be fathers are having the strange pregnancy symptoms they may be sharing with their pregnant partners.

Another field of interest that P. A. Simon explores through his writing is family budgeting and personal money management. Based on his experiences in life as an involved father and husband, as well as his profound understanding of economics, especially budgeting, he has also devoted significant attention to household budgeting. His short e-book *"Family budgeting: Guide to Managing Household Finance"* was written to help families make the best use of the money they have, and ensure proper management of their finances without major hiccups due to overspending.

He just finished his fourth book on personal finance which will provide excellent tips for individuals with low income to help them manage their finances effectively. Although he is not a professional in this field, his extensive experience with money management, both in times of crisis and abundance, has prepared him for many money-related disasters. He hopes to help his readers to be prepared as well.

These delightful books are fun to read and come right from the heart of someone who has experienced all of these things first-hand. They are his perspective on various aspects of family and parenthood, which would help his readers understand their familial commitments better and be in the best position to fulfill their responsibilities. Undoubtedly, the books are a true family necessity!

Apart from writing, P. A. Simon is a father who passionately devotes his free time to his son, cooking, engaging in physical activities (he loves running and plays volleyball in an amateur league), and acquiring more knowledge in the field of economy and child psychology.

www.ingramcontent.com/pod-product-compliance
Lightning Source LLC
LaVergne TN
LVHW010518200726
843506LV00013B/2631